Leadership Communication in Theory and Practice

MARIANNE WOLFF LUNDHOLT AND ANETTE ULDALL

Leadership Communication in Theory and Practice

Samfundslitteratur

Marianne Wolff Lundholt and Anette Uldall
Leadership Communication in Theory and Practice

1st edition, 2nd print run 2024

© The authors and Samfundslitteratur 2019

Editor: Henrik Schjerning
Copy Editor: Kevin Ploug Knudsen
Translation: Clem Luxford (CML Translation Ltd.)
Cover: Lonnie Hamborg (Imperiet)
Typeset: Steen Christensen, SL grafik (slgrafik.dk)
The book is set in Franklin Gothic and Minion Pro
Print: cpi-print

Publication of this book has been financially supported by BRANDBASE

ISBN: 978-87-593-3296-2

PEER REVIEWED

Samfundslitteratur
info@samfundslitteratur.dk
samfundslitteratur.dk

All rights reserved. No part of this publication may be reproduced by institutions or companies without prior agreement with Copydan Writing, and then only within the provisions of the agreement. Brief extracts for review are excepted.

Contents

Preface	**9**
The aim of the book	11
A bit about the book's structure	12
Who is the book for?	14
Thank you	15

Part I: Theory
By Marianne Wolff Lundholt

Chapter 1
An introduction to leadership communication	**19**
The book's foundation	20
The three types of appeal	21
Communication paradigms	25
The ten paradoxes of leadership communication	28

Chapter 2
What is leadership communication?	**31**
Management versus leadership communication	31
One definition of leadership communication: more than just communication from the boss	34

Chapter 3
Leadership communication – a complex task	**39**
Why is it so difficult?	39
All understanding is based on a preconception	40
Cascade communication	44
Middle manager's communication task is complicated	50

Chapter 4
Leadership communication's three forms of communication   53
The potential of leadership communication   54
Leadership communication's three forms and paradigms   56

Chapter 5
Leadership communication as information   59
Did you receive my message?   60
The information paradigm's communication understanding   61
When the message is formulated in advance of the communication   62
Employee satisfaction survey: Have you been informed?   62
The legitimacy of the information paradigm   63
Limitations of the information paradigm   65

Chapter 6
Leadership communication as communication   67
Did you understand my message?   67
The communication paradigm's communication understanding   68
Employee satisfaction survey: just an indication?   69
The legitimacy of the communication paradigm   69
Limitations of the communication paradigm   70

Chapter 7
Leadership communication as involvement   75
How do you understand the message?   76
The involvement paradigm's communication understanding   76
When the message is formulated in the communication situation   77
Employee satisfaction survey: Does it make sense?   80
The legitimacy of the involvement paradigm   80
Limitations of the involvement paradigm   82

Chapter 8
Leadership communication and communication environment — 85
- The organization's communication environment — 85
- Measurement of the communication environment — 96
- The road to an open communication environment — 97

Part II: From theory to practice
By Anette Uldall

Chapter 9
The Leadership Communication Tool Kit — 103
- Communication's seven elements — 103
- A tool kit for an internal communication strategy — 121

Chapter 10
Training gives leadership communication a boost — 127
- Step-by-step communication training — 128
- Planning and implementation of communication training — 132

Chapter 11
Case: When the new strategy requires new communication skills — 135
- Step 1: The strategy is launched — 136
- Step 2: Cascade communication — 139
- Step 3: Example of leadership communication in a business division — 142

Part III: Conclusion
By Marianne Wolff Lundholt and Anette Uldall

Conclusion — 151

Bibliography — 157

Preface

Numerous studies show that the immediate manager is the primary communication channel when communicating strategic messages to employees. The question is, how do we best tackle this task? Many of the communication challenges that managers face are classic, recurring problems. For instance, the challenge could be to create a common understanding of the strategy. Or to get employees to take ownership of the strategy, even though they are rarely involved in devising it. Finally, it's an enormous task for managers to meet employees' daily need for information and communication.

The City of Odense, a larger Danish city, has spent years working on a comprehensive transformation. The Communication Department conducted a series of focus group interviews with people managers. The result showed that people managers experienced the following challenges with internal communication:

- Busyness and scarce resources limit the support and understanding of the transformation. Their core tasks are perceived as more critical, and the transformation is seen as an extra and unnecessary layer that managers feel they must shield employees from.
- Different views of the transformation affect communication across the administration and management layers.
- Managers often feel that the information on the transformation from their immediate manager is insufficient and the line of communication is generally perceived as unreliable.
- There is a lack of general and accessible information about the transformation and its significance for the individual employee.
- The underlying message and the transformation need to be communicated through more channels than merely via the intranet.

- Managers require visual communication, excellent and specific examples, objective images, materials that can support employees in their core duties, an idea bank for managers – including exercises that help with presentations, and questions that can be asked at staff meetings, etc.

It's our experience that such issues are high on the agenda in Communication Departments in all types of organizations.

In this book, we will show you that the road to better leadership communication is about thinking of communication in a more nuanced way, so it's not just going to be about getting the messages "cascaded" or "rolled out". Studies show that managers tend to perceive communication as a series of messages to be channelled into the organization. This communication understanding is not necessarily incorrect. The problem arises when, as a manager, you expect that a cascade of messages automatically implies ownership and commitment among employees. If that is the goal of communication, then other forms of communication must also be used.

Another challenge is that as a manager, we tend to downgrade the leadership communication task despite recognizing its importance. Studies show that managers don't consider communication important enough to be prioritized over other tasks (O'Murchú 2015: 99). It's an unfortunate trend because communication is the key to action and execution (O'Rourke 2014). In other words, communication is a vital leadership tool.

Finally, as a manager, we tend to underestimate how long it takes to fulfil the goal of communication. If the goal is to get employees to *take ownership* of a strategic decision, there is a need for a more time-consuming process than if the goal is merely to *inform* them of a given message. If, for example, it's a case of a major round of redundancies, where several hundred employees are to be laid off, it's essential that managers are equipped to handle the task. There is an extensive and time-consuming task here that precedes the communication itself.

The aim of the book

In our work with leadership communication, we sadly missed a book that could give us an overview of the theories in the field. We also learned that when you work with both professional and non-professional communicators, it's a great advantage to speak the same language and create a common understanding of what leadership communication is. Plenty of literature has been written by and for practitioners, but with this book we want to contribute with specific examples of how you can effectively transform leadership communication from theory to practice. We will draw on existing research and our own experiences as communication advisors and consultants in all types of organizations (private and public organizations, as well as NGOs).

Leadership communication essentially consists of communication between employees and managers. It has been demonstrated that it's not entirely straightforward to define the area, although many have tried. In this book, we will give our take on how the area can be defined, and not least how the definition and demarcation can be associated with practical use (see Chapter 2). The reason so many attempts have been made to define leadership communication is it may be debatable whether leadership communication is actually an independent discipline, or whether it's a particular area within organizational communication or strategic communication.

We *don't* want to take our starting point in this book in specific communication areas. We would rather highlight some of the basic elements of leadership communication and so demonstrate that good leadership communication is not only about choosing the right channels! Good leadership communication goes much deeper than that. We define leadership communication as *the communication related means that a manager uses to achieve a specific purpose*. The essence of leadership communication is that in every communication situation you must compare the purpose of the communication (what do I want to achieve with the communication?) against the form of communication (what type of communication can meet this goal?). This reflection requires an understanding of what is possible to achieve through the various forms of communication.

There are also other important parameters that come into play. What is the sender's relationship with the recipient? What are the consequences of the message for the recipient? And what is the communication environment like in the department and the organization? If an organization has an open communication environment where managers at all levels appreciate employee feedback, and where there is confidence in management, then even the least engaging media (such as online media) can act as a good focal point for a valuable conversation. At the same time, organizations with a more closed communication environment have negative experiences with creating dialogue even at so-called dialogue meetings where you sit face-to-face and are well placed for a candid conversation.

So, the focal point of the book is to highlight the forms of communication that support which communication objectives and also create an awareness of the mechanisms that underlie these synergies.

The content was selected on the basis to support the purpose of the book. This means that the book contains both traditional and more recent theories of communication. Common to these theories is that, to a greater or lesser extent, they help to sharpen our understanding of the forms of communication that support the communication objective.

A bit about the book's structure

The book is divided into two parts: a theoretical part and a practical one. Part I provides an overview of theories within leadership communication, and Part II gives examples of how this knowledge can be translated into practice. Since the practical part is based on cases and is not originally designed with the purpose of illustrating the theoretical part, there will be some theory parts that have more space than others. Overall, the cases serve to illustrate how forms of communication can be combined in practice and support various communication purposes.

Chapter 1 provides an introduction to the concept of "leadership communication" and the potential that lies in working professionally with this discipline. The chapter begins by looking back on rhetoric and domain theory to show why it's relevant to work based on three different communication paradigms when working with leadership communication. We have also briefly described how this book differs from other books on leadership communication, and to whom it's aimed at. Finally, we introduce the *ten paradoxes of leadership communication*.

In Chapter 2, we go one step further and give a true definition of leadership communication. Here we also present leadership communication's three forms of communication: *transmission, dialogue and involvement.*

Chapter 3 is about the many factors that make leadership communications a challenging task.

In Chapters 4-7, the three communication paradigms – *information, communication and involvement* – and the forms of communication – transmission, dialogue and involvement – are reviewed and linked to general communication theory. The purpose of these chapters is to show how and when managers can use the three forms of communication and paradigms to achieve the goal of communication and increase the chances of succeeding in the task.

Chapter 8 discusses what creates and prevents an open communication environment. Based on research in this area, we point out some key mechanisms that come into play in relation to the motivation of management and employees to maintain a closed communication environment and its likely consequences. We will also suggest how to gain insight into whether the communication environment is open or closed.

Then we go from theory to practice. A good tool kit is always a help, and therefore we introduce a simple and effective communication tool, the "Leadership Communication Tool Kit", which we have jointly developed. The tool kit has been used by hundreds of managers who have been trained to use the seven elements in the box. In short, it's about going through a process where the user considers the target group and objective – including the form of communication, message, anticipated reactions, channels, timing and responsibility for the communication. The ultimate goal is to adjust the message to the target group, which is crucial in order to succeed in your leadership communication. It's our experience that managers with this tool in hand are more effective and targeted in their preparations. They will be able to both plan a specific communication and devise a communication strategy for the organization, while they also develop their own communication skills.

Chapter 9 shows how the tool kit can be used to plan a specific communication task and discusses how it can be used to devise a communication strategy.

In Chapter 10, we review an example of how to train managers in leadership communication using the "Leadership Communication Tool Kit".

Chapter 11 is a case from Danfoss that can be used as inspiration to improve managers' communication skills. Danfoss is a global company within the energy technology sector. The case is based on the introduction of Danfoss' "Core & Clear" strategy.

Finally, in "Conclusion" we provide a summary of the book's main points.

The bibliography can be used as inspiration to continue working with relevant themes.

Who is the book for?

In many cases, a manager has had no communication training and so, as a starting point, they don't have the necessary knowledge and skills to perform the task professionally.

Therefore, leadership communication is perceived by many managers as "something you just do". The consequence may be that you don't see your own inadequacies in situations where communication fails because you don't have the skills to reflect professionally about how to tackle the communication. Often the manager will see employees as the cause of the problem. Perceptions of employees who are not sufficiently "ready for change" or "agile" can come to influence the manager's relationship with their employees, and it will reduce the chances of success for the leadership communication.

It's our intention with this book to provide managers in all types of organizations – private and listed companies, NGOs and government organizations – not trained in communications, with an insight into the theory that forms the basis of leadership communication. We believe that the more knowledge and common language that trained and non-communication trained employees share, the more likely it is that you can improve the communication environment while also increasing job satisfaction and the organization's business performance. In addition to providing a theoretical foundation, the book contributes specific tools to help the manager achieve a more professional approach to the task with leadership communication.

The book is also aimed at communication consultants and students, as it provides an overview of the essential elements of leadership communication and crucial insight into the complexity of the discipline. With this mixed target group of theorists and practitioners in mind, we have decided to put some of the conceptually heavy parts of the text into text boxes. This allows the non-theoretical reader to easily skip the theory without missing the point of the book.

Thank you

We would like to thank our collaborators who have taken the time to discuss, give feedback and support this publication.

Thank you to our editor from Samfundslitteratur, Henrik Schjerning, for a highly professional and rewarding collaboration. Thanks to Peter Stray Jørgensen for constructive feedback on the linguistic processing. Also, thank you to Mette Refshauge and Jesper Løv for interesting conversations and collaboration on leadership communication. We would also like to thank Susanne Kjærbeck for her constructive input.

Thanks to Jens Degn and Mette Schnefeld for their inspiring conversations, valuable comments and contribution to the cases. Mette has also helped to think of the first ideas about the Leadership Communication Tool Kit. This idea development was done in collaboration with Peter

Braun, who was helpful in preparing processes and materials associated with the communication training.

Thank you to Thomas Holluf Nielsen and Betina Stage for an exciting collaboration with Domea.dk about the "Counter-narratives in organizations" research project. The project has generated powerful insights into leadership communication that we continually draw on in this book.

Also thanks to Kjeld Stærk, Ole Møller-Jensen, Troels H. Petersen, Hans Peter Boisen and Ole Daugbjerg for having confidence in our joint work with leadership communication in practice at Danfoss and also to challenge us to be more focused on discipline.

Thank you to our former communication colleagues Sally Foster-Mortensen and Lisa Pilgaard, who have been together with us on the journey and who continue to work to support leadership communication at Danfoss.

Finally, we wish to thank BRANDBASE for supporting the translation and production of the book.

As the above list shows, many of our sources of inspiration have their roots at Danfoss. As the book not only draws on research but also on our own practical experience, a lot of our cases are inspired by our work with leadership communication in this context.

Part I: Theory

By Marianne Wolff Lundholt

Chapter 1
An introduction to leadership communication

> Leadership occurs through the process of interaction and communication. (Barge and Hirokawa 1989: 172)

The fact that management and communication are closely linked is no longer up for discussion either in academia or among practitioners. Formulations such as "Management is communication", "Communication is the key to good management" and "Managers use 80% of their working time to communicate" resonates in most management teams today. Also, in executive management offices, communication is linked with the company's success, according to a study (Zerfass and Sherzada 2015). The same study also shows that internal communication between employees and managers is considered the most important discipline within corporate communication, followed by marketing, communication with customers and financial communication (ibid.: 302). The reason for the increased focus on communication is the awareness that internal, as well as external communication, is essential in relation to the organization's performance (Marques 2010: 50). In fact, Riel (2016) proclaims that leadership communication is the most important form of communication in an organization and considers managers' communication skills as one of the essential skills when a manager must create support for organizational goals.

The numerous further education courses in communication testify that communication is one of the areas where a lot of resources are being used in terms of both time and money. Communication courses typically focus on how to get your message "through" – either in various media or in relation to a management team, employees and other stakeholders. Presentation technique is one of the skills highlighted as particularly central. Experts in the past have given many suggestions for what percentage of communication is body language, tone of voice and words (see, for example, Mehrabian 1981). "Personal impact" is also one of the many buzzwords often associated with communication competence, not to mention the courses to focus and streamline communication.

The fact that leadership communication has great potential is underpinned by the many studies over the years that have put a monetary figure on the value of communication within organizations. For example, a US study describes how 1 in 5 projects fail because of ineffective communication within the organization, which means that a significant proportion of the amount invested in these projects runs the risk of being lost (Project Management Institute 2013).

Studies have also shown that there is a close correlation between communication and employee satisfaction. Some theorists have even spoken of "commitment communication" (see, for instance, Welch, 2015). Well-informed employees feel valued, and it creates commitment and motivation. Increased employee commitment is of high economic value as it contributes to growth, profit, productivity and employee retention (Harter et al. 2002).

Overall, we can conclude that there is great potential in working professionally with leadership communication. The only question is why organizations are still lagging behind when it comes to optimizing their communication. There may, of course, be many explanations for this. In addition to leadership communication being a hugely demanding discipline merely because it involves communication between people, a vital explanation is that the task of leadership communication is often handled by managers not trained in communication.

The book's foundation

As mentioned in the introduction, the essence of leadership communication is that in any communication situation you must keep to the objective of the communication (What do I want to achieve with communication?), against the form of communication (What type of communication can meet this goal?). This reflection requires an understanding of what is possible to achieve through the various forms of communication.

There has been work within traditional rhetoric on ways that may appeal to your recipient using the different modes of language based on philosopher Aristotle's *Rhetoric*. Here you work with 3 basic forms of appeal, which each have their strengths and weaknesses. To show why it's crucial that you are aware of which communication objectives the chosen form of communication can and must achieve, we will provide a brief introduction to the appeal forms in the following section. The section will be followed by a review of the so-called domain theory, which shows that our way of talking about things can be linked to a specific logic. The two sections are a warm-up to the section on communication paradigms, which is the book's foundation.

The three types of appeal

The three types of appeal are called "ethos", "pathos" and "logos". The types of appeal refer to the means the sender has at their disposal to persuade the recipient of their message. The three types of appeal are typically all present in a communication situation, but there is usually one that is more prominent.

With *ethos*, you appeal to the recipient's trust towards the sender. When the sender is trustworthy – seen from the recipient's eyes – you can base your message on the trust established between the manager and employees. If there is trust between the manager and employees, the manager has a strong foundation for communication because employees are generally not as critical of the message. If you have not yet built up this trust, then via the other types of appeal and through body language and the way to make your point in time, the manager can gain credibility and so establish a relationship of trust. Of course, employees assess the manager on *what* they say, but what matters first and foremost is that the manager *complies* with what they say. The manager can generally build up their credibility through three virtues:

- By showing that they are a knowledgeable, intelligent and experienced person ("I've been a manager at the company for the last 20 years").
- By showing that they have a good moral character ("It's important to me that my employees thrive").
- By showing your goodwill and meeting your audience halfway ("I understand why you are sceptical about the new strategy").

You can also strengthen your ethos by referring to other credible sources, for example, experts, the board or senior management. In this way, you "borrow" others' credibility by showing that they have the same opinions.

With *pathos*, the sender tries to convince the recipient by appealing to the recipient's emotions, both in the choice of often value-laden words and the way the message is conveyed. The recipient will experience the sender as someone who "speaks from the heart". It may be emotions that arouse anger, joy, disgust, hatred or commitment. In some cultures, pathos is a vital part of the way people communicate. In other parts of the world there is a risk that it appears unreliable, even comical if you exaggerate the use of pathos, and then the message falls on deaf ears. Pathos can have a powerful effect as long as it's used in the proper doses depending on the communication situation and recipient. At the same time, you can say that the right dose of pathos can get the message to appear more authentic because you "speak from the heart". As more and more managers participate in communication training, their form of communication can appear very polished and articulate, but also a little distant. This effect is enhanced if communication is conveyed using many PowerPoint slides that the sender often hasn't prepared himself.

Logos appeals to the recipient's common sense and uses an objective type of language. It's this type of appeal that is often dominant in leadership communication. Using logos, the sender is trying to appeal to the recipient's common sense by using logical arguments in their message. Claims are substantiated by evidence in the form of presenting objective evidence such as statistics and studies or customer/employee satisfaction surveys.

Logos' strength is when it comes to convincing the recipient of the legitimacy of the message/decision. At the same time, it reflects the communication situation where something is either right or wrong, true or false. The formulations are linked together as cause-effect. This means that communication often takes the form of the following three elements:

- Wish ("Our goal is …").
- Cause ("Therefore, we must …").
- Effect ("Then we can achieve …").

This logos-orientated way of formulating reflects an idea that there is one objective reality. This reality is put into play through the cause-effect mindset. So, if we do X (for example efficiency), then Y (for example increased earnings) happens. You can often recognize this form of communication in expressions like "since", "because", "therefore", "that is to say", "it's because of", "as a result of".

The idea is that management identifies a problem and a solution and then communicates both the problem and solution to the employees.

As a recipient, the focus will be to *remember* and *understand* the messages, so the recipient can convey it to the next levels in the organization. Despite the fact that a vision has much more potential in increasing employees' engagement, management often tends to focus on financial goals in their leadership communication (for example increased earnings) rather than starting with their vision (for example to create the most attractive homes).

The three types of appeal may be more or less dominant in different situations in which communication takes place. It's important for a manager to be aware of the prevailing context in the communication situation, as it influences communication and understanding of a given message. If we take a look at biologists Humberto Maturana and Francisco Varela's domain theory, we can distinguish between different types of context called "domains".

Domain theory

Domain theory visualizes that our way of talking about things can be linked to a specific logic. Maturana and Varela (1987) distinguish between three such domains: reflection, aesthetics and production domain.

The *reflection domain* is characterized by the existence of many versions of reality rather than one final truth. This leads to an openness to many different interpretations of the messages. The focus is on diversity and to explore how emotions, thoughts and actions affect and are affected by others. In the reflection domain, you reflect freely and explore the many versions of reality.

In the *aesthetics domain*, the focal point is the communicating parties' emotions, values, morals, as well as relationships and attitudes to ethical issues.

In the *production domain*, the form of communication is based on the fact that there is only one reality. The communication aims to solve the problems facing the organization at that time – with a focus on action based on clarity of, for example, processes and workflows. Therefore, communication must generally be effective in the sense that the messages need to be communicated uninterrupted from the manager to employees. The form of communication in the production domain is the rational and argumentative form of communication, which is primarily dominated by the logos type of appeal.

It's vital to point out that none of the three types of appeal or the three domains is more "right" or "wrong" than the others. It's only important that you are aware of which communication objectives the chosen form of communication can and must achieve. The production domain is, for instance, essential in terms of giving guidance to individual employees such as communication policies, ethics or other common rules.

All three domains are usually in play when we communicate. However, just like types of appeals, there is typically one domain that is more prominent than the other two. The dominant domain characterizes not just the way the sender communicates, but also the recipient's expectations of the communication.

Communication problems may be due to the manager speaking based on one domain and the employee from another. Or the manager is primarily in one domain but pretends to be in another.

We see an example of this in the following excerpt from a "soapbox meeting" where the CEO invites reflection in a final dialogue session with an employee following a protracted review of the organization's strategic initiatives and ambitions primarily put forward as arguments in the production domain:

 CEO: It's the ambitions we work with that we must succeed with and document before the end of the first half of 2018. Do you recognize that?

Unknown man: Yes.

CEO: Good. How far are we? (Soapbox meeting 2016)

In terms of content, the question "Do you recognize that?" is a reflection question. However, yes/no questions reflect the production domain and focus on getting employees to understand the message rather than relating reflectively to the content, i.e., take a position on it. Therefore, the CEO gets no awareness of *what* it is the employee in question recognizes. You could say that the form of language creates a kind of contract between the sender and recipient as there is no invitation to dialogue, but rather the recipient assumes the role of a listening audience that seeks to understand the messages.

There is no doubt that the production domain and its argumentative logos-orientated form of communication are dominant in many organizations. If the goal of communication is to achieve more than just a rational understanding of a message, it requires that the manager can use more dialogic and involving forms of communication.

Communication paradigms

That the manager can distinguish between different forms of communication determines whether the communication is successful or not.

In this book, we therefore work based on Nielsen's (2014) three communication paradigms:

1. Information: asymmetrical one-way communication that aims to gain knowledge and acceptance.
2. Communication: asymmetrical two-way communication with some degree of involvement of feedback from the recipient to gain understanding.
3. Involvement: symmetrical two-way communication or dialogue, including involvement and communication via others to achieve ownership (42).

By "paradigm" we mean the way we look at something – in this case, communication. The three paradigms are defined, amongst other things, based on the concept of dialogue in relation to whether it's a case of one-way or two-way communication. However, there are not three sharply defined forms of dialogue. This means that although the information paradigm is characterized by one-way communication, communication within this paradigm may well be based on dialogue. A manager can, for instance, be in dialogue with an employee in relation to whether the employee has received the message or not. Similarly, dialogue is fundamental to both the communication paradigm *and* the involvement paradigm.

It's our experience that in the practical work of leadership communication, you often focus on whether employees have received and/or understood the message (including the many strategy workshops that both managers and employees spend many resources on), but don't emphasize involvement to the same degree in order to create a new common understanding. The task in the involvement paradigm is not to simply transmit a final message to the employees or to get employees to understand a message. Rather, it's a question of establishing a communication environment where involvement can occur. The employees here are not just considered as passive recipients of strategic messages, but instead, they play an active role in relation to the interpretation process (Larson and Pepper 2003). It's precisely this process that is the focal point of the involvement paradigm. The challenge here is not that we *lack* information, but instead that there are so many opportunities to create meaning (Hammer and Høpner 2014: 102). Therefore, a key task is that both the manager and the employees work with a common understanding of a message if the goal of the communication is to create ownership. In the book, we will explain some of the key, underlying mechanisms in relation to the involvement paradigm, while at the same time providing some specific tools for how managers can work within the paradigm. Since our focus is on leadership communication, it's not our aim to give our take on different forms of involvement processes that are traditionally considered part of the HR toolbox. We will, however, stay focused on communication itself.

The following table shows how the three communication paradigms are expressed in the associated forms of communication:

	Communication form	Communication paradigm
1	Transmission: One-way communication from the manager to employees	The information paradigm
2	Dialogue: Dialogic communication between the manager and employees	The communication paradigm
3	Involvement: The involvement of employees	The involvement paradigm

As mentioned, there are three defined forms of communication, as dialogue can be the focal point for all three categories. In reference works, dialogue is often defined as a conversation between two or more people. Research-based definitions also point to dialogue as an act that aims to build bridges across differences (Phillips 2011), or to achieve a common objective (Tsoukas 2009). The dialogic process behind building a bridge or attain a common understanding may take different forms. As Foster and Jonker (2005) show, dialogue can serve two different purposes. The dialogue, in what we call the communication paradigm, aims to give the sender feedback, which they can use to adjust the message, so the recipient better understands what the sender is trying to say. The aim here is to achieve a common understanding of the *sender's* message. In the involvement paradigm, the dialogue serves a purpose to involve employees, so they can help to formulate A, B and the path from A to B (Nielsen 2014: 37). The focus here is on *both* the sender and recipient, both of whom are active in relation to forming the message's content with a starting point in the parties' different understandings. Therefore, the dialogue concept has different meanings in different forms of communication.

The ten paradoxes of leadership communication

The communication paradigms and forms are fundamental in leadership communication. Using these paradigms might give rise to a number of paradoxes you as a leader might encounter in your daily work with leadership communication. We call them "The ten paradoxes of leadership communication":

1. To invite feedback, BUT never get a response.
2. To get feedback, BUT not have the time to engage in dialogue.
3. Communicated the message, BUT desired effect not achieved in the target group.
4. Knowing your target group, BUT still being surprised by their reactions.
5. Having limited time to communicate, BUT spending a lot of time on e-mails.
6. Argumentation using facts, BUT only achieving understanding rather than commitment.
7. Having control over the message, BUT being unable to relinquish control and listen in dialogue with employees.

8. Assessing that communication is relevant, BUT for whom?
9. Communicating in a world of communication noise, BUT not just "shouting louder".
10. Having to communicate senior management's message, BUT not being convinced that it makes sense.

If you recognize one or more of the statements, then you can calmly read on! The book will try to give inspiration to working with leadership communication so that the ten paradoxes no longer lead to an inability to act.

Chapter 2
What is leadership communication?

The many disciplines and skills within communication in organizations are testimony that the discipline of communication is wide-ranging. The question is how the concept of "leadership communication" must be defined and kept separate from other communication disciplines. In this chapter, we will examine how the concept has been defined and applied.

In general, we talk about management, both when it comes to the more mechanical and often slightly more immediate task to manage, control and measure an organization's activities, and when it's about the long-term, more strategic work that also to a high degree includes ensuring motivation and commitment. However, the nuances are better covered by the two separate terms "management" and "leadership".

When it comes to leadership communication, it makes excellent sense to take a closer look at the differences, since the two types of tasks require entirely different communication skills and therefore different tools. We will then examine the concepts of "strategic leadership communication" and "leadership communication". The chapter will end with the book's definition of leadership communication.

Management versus leadership communication

Overall, management is a task where communication is a tool that managers must use to support employees in the performance of their duties. Communication in a leadership perspective is more about building trust between managers and employees, where a vital goal is to ensure employee commitment and support for the corporate strategy.

In principle, it makes good sense to maintain this distinction between "leadership" and "management" because they relate to different communication tasks. However, there is a tendency that the difference between the two concepts gets blurred when they are connected with communication. This is because the concept of "management" in many theoretical contexts is used to describe leadership in a broad sense. This, in turn, means that most theorists and scholars use the term "management communication" as an overall term for the communication activities that are carried out, regardless of whether it's a case of leadership or management. "Leadership communication" becomes a label that is put on managers' communication with employees and the dialogue that can be created internally between management levels and employees. The designation helps to separate leadership communication from the many other communication disciplines that are in play in a modern organization.

Definitions of leadership communication

The research presents a different proposal of how leadership communication must be defined. One suggestion is to distinguish four domains in internal communication:

1. Business (communication skills among employees).
2. Corporate (the formal communication typically devised by the Communication Department).
3. Organizational (communication's opinion-forming).
4. Management communication (the manager's communication skills) (Kalla 2005).

Management communication here is about developing and spreading knowledge within the organization with a focus on increasing the efficiency of the organization's employees. Communication is considered as a set of skills that can be improved by using the prescribed guidelines.

Another way to define leadership communication is to consider management communication as a discipline that extends beyond a range of communication skills (Riel and Fombrun 2007). Management communication is categorized as one of three disciplines of corporate communication:

1. Management communication.
2. Marketing communication.
3. Organizational communication.

Management communication is described here as communication from management, which aims to achieve a shared vision, establish and maintain confidence in the management, manage change and to strengthen employee motivation and empowerment.

The fusion between "leadership" and "management communication" is particularly evident in the following understanding of "management communication", where the concept is perceived as a task in facilitating activities and creating understanding of the organization's mission, vision and goals, and to also give employees information on day-to-day activities (Hallahan et al. 2007). The concept of "management communication" is also used as a common name for both management and leadership communication (Cornelissen 2017). With the concept of "employee communication", Cornelissen distinguishes between:

1. Management communication (communication related to each employee's specific tasks and activities and their morale and well-being).
2. Corporate information and communication systems (the technological communication systems that make the first category possible, and the cascading of overall messages within the organization).

There are many examples of this distinction between "leadership" and "management communication" creeping into the language. There is, however, far from a disciplined use of the concepts. In a newsletter from the Danish Managers' Competence Centre (*Ledernes Kompetencecenter*), the title, for example, read as follows: "Strengthen your leadership with a communication course" (2017). Despite the emphasis on "leadership", the aim of the course was described in the body of the newsletter as follows: "Penetrate with effective communication and activate your recipients". The communication course is about both learning what you can categorize as management communication (i.e., communication in practice that deals with purposeful and effective communication) and leadership communication (i.e., communication between managers and employees with a focus on commitment, dialogue and feedback).

In Danish literature, leadership communication is portrayed as a phenomenon that many have an opinion on, but few have defined and so limited to an independent discipline. It's surprising to see how many contributors to books on the area – even with leadership communication as part of the title – refrain from giving readers a precise definition of the concept.

An example is the book *Transformational leadership communication – metaphors in organizations* (2012). Here, the authors, Linda Greve and Steen Hildebrandt, give a fascinating description of how our way of thinking and talking about communication and organizations in the form of metaphors can create change. Transformational leadership communication is about "identifying the images the organization thinks of as routines, visions and opportunities, and then change them in the direction that will be meaningful" (ibid.: 8). A proper definition of leadership communication doesn't exist.

Only a few Danish theorists have historically given their take on how to distinguish between the different communication disciplines within organizations. It's interesting here to see that there are generally two different concepts, namely "leadership communication" and "strategic leadership communication".

"Strategic leadership communication" is defined as "leadership with vision, mission and values" (Bordum 2016: 269). Strategic leadership communication here is about "circumstances that play an important role in defining and creating a deliberate and coordinated development direction of a company" (ibid.). The focus here is on integrating the development and formulation of the strategy with strategic communication, so you as a manager are able to create a strategic direction for the company.

In this context, a clear and well-formulated business strategy is essential for the strategic communication work (Argenti 2017), which aims to anchor communication in the corporate strategy. The following definition of leadership communication is particularly interesting as it embraces the establishment of relationships between the communicating parties in a leadership context as the focal point for leadership communication, rather than the actual communication message. Erik Johnsen defines leadership communication as to "create, maintain, develop and handle relations between people who exercise management behaviour" (Johnsen 2003: 174).

Communication is not just a matter of passing on a message; it's also a question of creating, maintaining or changing relationships. This means that a change of communication can affect the relationship. This is a crucial point that leadership communication manages to embrace because it focuses on the longer-term strategic effects of communication. Management communication, in contrast, takes its starting point in a specific message, which is the objective itself here and now. Both communication objectives are relevant. What matters is whether you as a manager can adapt your form of communication in relation to what you want to achieve.

One definition of leadership communication: more than just communication from the boss

In this book, the concept of "leadership communication" covers both leadership and management communication. This embraces leadership communication, both what we have introduced as strategic leadership communication and as management communication. It's not sufficient to define leadership communication just as a matter of "spreading knowledge within the organization". Such a formulation reflects an understanding of leadership communication as information to be cascaded or rolled out in the organization.

Defining leadership communication as "communication from management" is also unfortunate because it may give the impression that leadership communication is limited to one-way communication *from* the manager to employees (see the information paradigm). It's insufficient if it's a *dialogue* between employees and management you are looking for (see the communication paradigm). Finally, it's a prerequisite for achieving employee ownership that in the dialogue the manager is also able to get *involved* and *create meaning in the interaction with employees* (see the involvement paradigm). It's precisely these three fundamental parts of leadership communication that this book takes as its starting point:

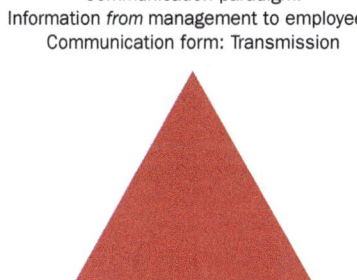

Communication paradigm:
Information *from* management to employees
Communication form: Transmission

Communication paradigm:
Communication *between*
employees and management
Communication form: Dialogue

Communication paradigm:
Employee involvement
Communication form: Involvement

Figure 1. The three communication paradigms/forms of leadership communication.

The fact that leadership communication contains these three communication paradigms/forms is an important recognition if you want to succeed in your communication. It's precisely the ability to evaluate and choose the right form of communication where a large part of the key to good leadership communication can be found.

If the message is relatively straightforward and the purpose of the communication is to inform, communication from management to employees may be sufficient. If it's about changing opinions and behaviour, which will typically be the case in change projects and strategic tasks, it's important to use a dialogue-based approach to the communication task. Motivation in the most profound form requires more. It's crucial here that the manager in the dialogue creates room for interpretation, where employees can interpret the messages so that the employees, together with management, are part of the solution. Then we move over into the involvement paradigm.

Hallahan et al. (2007), defines, as mentioned, leadership communication as a task in facilitating activities and creating an understanding of the organization's mission, vision and goals, and also in giving employees information about day-to-day activities. This definition includes all three forms of communication: To provide employees with information will typically take the form of *transmission* from management to the employees, whereas to facilitate and create understanding is further achieved through *dialogue* between employees and management, and finally *involvement* as a form of communication when it comes to employees taking ownership.

Hallahan et al.'s definition of leadership communication embraces all three forms of communication, and we have therefore decided to take our starting point in this definition. However, we would like to add a single element: "ownership". To achieve the full effect of the messages, it's not sufficient that employees merely *understand* the messages. Employees must make the messages their own, so any changes make sense to them. With employee ownership, it increases the likelihood that management actually obtains employee acceptance of the messages, and in turn, achieves a greater business-related impact.

We are now approaching a comprehensive definition of the concept of "leadership communication". Generally, we understand leadership communication as *the communication-related means that a manager uses to achieve a specific purpose.* This purpose can be strategic (leadership) and/or operational (management). Therefore, we will expand our definition of "leadership communication" with an extra level that embraces both elements, based on an adaptation of Hallahan et al.'s definition:

> Leadership communication is understood as a task to give employees information about day-to-day activities (management communication) and facilitate activities and/or create understanding and ownership of the organization's strategy (leadership communication).

In addition to adding ownership in relation to Hallahan et al.'s original definition, we have also replaced "mission, vision and goals" with "strategy" as the first-mentioned concepts are not as widespread as before. Today, for example, many organizations have replaced mission and vision with "value proposition", which, as a starting point, is more customer-orientated.

We return to the definition in Chapter 4, where we examine leadership communication's three forms of communication.

Chapter 3

Leadership communication – a complex task

In the previous chapter, we defined leadership communication as a strategic task (to facilitate activities and create understanding and ownership of the organization's strategy) and an operational task (to give employees information about day-to-day activities). In this chapter, we will look at some of the issues you as a manager often encounter in your daily work with leadership communication and why they occur. We will touch upon key areas such as the subjective interpretation process, cascade communication, relevance communication and the difficult communication role of middle managers.

Why is it so difficult?

There is no doubt that managers face a complex job when it comes to communicating. Although most managers understand the significance of leadership communication, many come up short in terms of how they actually communicate professionally.

Simple messages such as practical information, status, results or the like are typically not difficult to handle. However, sometimes the communication task requires much more of both managers and employees, and so the road can feel long and tortuous. If you ask employees to what extent they are satisfied with communication in their organization, it's extremely rare that you get a positive response. Managers and employees often express that communication in the organization is inadequate. On one the hand, they feel that they have been over-informed, and on the other hand, they feel that they lack knowledge about what is most important.

There's no simple answer to why leadership communication is such a complicated task. Part of the answer may be found in managers' perception of what their communication job is actually all about. There is a tendency that good leadership communication is a matter of the message being communicated clearly, so there are no misunderstandings.

However, this approach doesn't embrace the complexity of communication. It's all too easy to overlook the fact that the recipient of any communication situation interprets messages from their personal experience. As recipients in a communication situation, we are not just a piece of blank paper that can be filled with messages and then a correct understanding is automatically created. Quite the contrary, we interpret messages based on our own so-called *preconceptions*.

All understanding is based on a preconception

The concept of "preconceptions" refers to the perceptions/opinions that we as humans have built up over time and formed the basis of our personal background (i.e., our social background, culture, education, gender, religion, values, etc.) and previous experiences (for example, if, as an employee, you have experienced a similar situation). It's precisely this subjective process that helps to make a communication task complicated.

Seeing the world as yourself is an important acknowledgement to understand that the task of communication is complicated. The subjective interpretation process can mean that sometimes, as a manager, you are surprised how the same message can be interpreted differently among employees. As an example of how the same message can trigger different interpretations, we look at how senior management at Domea.dk presented their 2015 strategy to employees: A message from management that the IT systems were to be optimized, triggered fears of layoffs in one employee group, while other employees interpreted the change as an important step towards a more customer-orientated organization.

The interpretation of the message is affected by the individual employee's interest in the message and whether the message has a major or minor impact on their everyday lives. This means that as the sender, prior to the communication, you must build an understanding of the recipient, including the interests and opinions they may have in relation to the messages. All this will affect the recipient's response to the message.

With the concept of "sensemaking" (Weick 1995), we can describe this process as a matter of "enlarging" small clues to a meaningful unit. Figure 2 shows an image with a variety of elements (clues):

Figure 2. Sensemaking. Sergey Nivens/Shutterstock.com.

Our interpretation is built upon these clues. It can be both visual (the characters, the gears, the colours, clothing, etc.), but it may also be other elements that surround the entire image (the material, the frame, the wall, the hanging, etc.).

During a sensemaking workshop for managers, there was one manager who expressed that he had expected that the workshop would solely focus on communication and not management, as it was the Communication Department that had issued the invitation to the workshop. This was a clear example of we constantly interpret based on various clues – in this case, the profile of the person who sent the invitation.

Translating this knowledge on clues and interpretation to a leadership communication context, it's clear that employees don't relate to the message alone. On the contrary, many other clues are pulled into the machinery behind every interpretation process. It could be a strategy, previous messages communicated in other contexts or via other channels, rumours or the manager's mood and body language.

Employees interpretation of messages based on key clues in the organization was experienced by Mette Schnefeld, HR Business Partner at Danfoss, in connection with an acquisition of a Finnish company in 2014.

After the acquisition was communicated within the organization, all the messages were linked with the acquisition, also in situations where decisions or events had nothing to do with the acquisition. Mette Schnefeld says:

> The ordinary things going on in a company – people hand in their notice, making decisions, major or minor organizational changes take place, process optimization, revised procedures, new directives, etc. – were for a long time interpreted into the framework of the acquisition process. It meant that when management teams discussed the communication of even the smallest changes, there was always a discussion of how it would be perceived by the respective original organizations, and how it would be interpreted and construed in relation to the acquisition, integration, and how far we were in the integration process. So the interpretation of the messages was often influenced by how you related to the actual acquisition. It was also found that some employees had the direct opposite effect if you tried to communicate that the decision had nothing to do with the acquisition, namely that they were convinced that there was certainly a link.

As this quote shows, sensemaking is not a defined dimension, but a process that is based on our different horizons of understanding. However, it doesn't mean that we don't allow ourselves to be influenced by others' understanding. Sensemaking is a social activity in the sense that meaning is created both individually and together with others (Weick 1995).

Sensemaking – an individual and social activity

As shown, we interpret messages from our own subjective horizons of understanding. However, if we find that others have a different meaning of the same message, then we (may) adjust our own original interpretation.

To illustrate this point, we can use the picture from before in a little exercise, which has been used in connection with training managers in sensemaking: The managers are given a picture similar to the illustration on page 41.

The managers are first asked to reflect on the picture's significance individually. Then they reflect on the picture with a teammate. The point of the exercise is that managers experience how different their interpretations of the same picture are. This seems surprising, as the picture for the individual seems unequivocal and clear in the individual reflection. After dialogue with a teammate, the manager often has a new and adjusted experience of the picture.

The exercise gives managers two realizations: 1. How different messages can be interpreted, and 2. How you become aware of new interpretations that you hadn't assigned to the picture in the individual reflection. Based on input from others, you adjust your interpretation of the picture.

If we put these findings in relation to leadership communication, it means that employees both interpret messages individually and in interaction with colleagues. It happens automatically. This means that the informal communication that takes place by the coffee machine is a natural and necessary way for employees to create meaning.

We find another example of interpretation taking place whether management requests it or not, in a large Danish company where in connection with the implementation of a new strategy, the Executive Management hires a consultant to act as an agent of change in the strategy process. In the following focus group interviews with a management team, one of the managers subsequently reflects on the speculation the consultant gave rise to. It should be added that the employees' first meeting with the consultant was in his capacity as a speaker. Only later, was he employed as a consultant:

> At the time, he was just there as a speaker. After Roskilde, the bosses were suddenly told that he was now hired as a consultant for the interim six months, and he will work on establishing a back office for business customers. I can't remember what we called it at the time. Of course, Executive Management is allowed to, and there was no jiggery-pokery there.
>
> However, a mix of his behaviour and that Executive Management was never really precise in their communication to us in relation to what it exactly was he was to do, what mandate he had and what it meant in relation to the others. Because there were namely stories (laughter) wondering whether he was a future member of the Executive Management and that he might replace him or him? We all made up some exciting stories in a few weeks. (Interview with the management team 2016)

The reflection shows that the bosses in the management team in question automatically tried to find the *meaning* of the consultant's role. Executive Management failed to make it clear what mandate the consultant had and thereby lost the ability to influence the opinion formation in the desired direction. This gave rise to uncertainty and speculation.

It can be difficult to take account of the subjective and social interpretation process in the communication situation, especially when the messages must be sent to a large number of employees. Employee satisfaction surveys show that managers are far more satisfied with communication than employees. It can be an indication that the messages usually emanate from the top of the organization and should be channelled to employees through middle managers. This form of communication is called "cascade communication".

Cascade communication

The idea behind cascade communication is that managers cascade messages from level to level until everyone in the organization has received the messages:

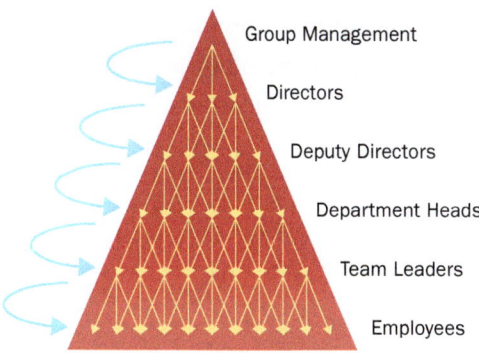

Figure 3. Cascade communication.

Cascade communication is also referred to as line communication and is about "information from management level to management level from the very top of the organization (group management) to the outermost part (ordinary employees)" (Petersen 2000: 72). The purpose of line communication is "to translate group management's messages, creating relevance from level to level." According to Helle Petersen, line communication is satisfactory "when it's just as reliable as the chain of command in the army – or when group management can confidently leave the communication of important messages to the line" (ibid.).

As senior management's role is to set the direction and communicate the overall messages within the organization, it makes sense to make use of the cascade model. The model gives the line manager the option to adjust messages in relation to their part of the organization. This allows the middle manager to maintain their management options, which would be difficult if senior management was alone responsible for communicating the messages for each department.

The limitations of cascade communication

Research shows that middle managers are the employees' most important communication channel (Larkin and Larkin 2006). Precisely for this reason, cascade communication makes sense in that the immediate manager acts as a communication channel for employees.

However, cascade communication may be difficult to rely on when the channelling of messages is often blocked very early in the process. Jesper Højberg Christensen has illustrated this problem with the following model:

Figure 4. Traditional top-down communication. Source: Adapted according to Christensen 2010.

The model shows how many middle managers tend to refrain from communicating messages to the next level. However, this only reflects one of the many problems associated with this form of communication. Other managers might choose to communicate only parts of the message in the organization, and finally, there are managers who have misunderstood the message – consciously or unconsciously. The model below illustrates the problem:

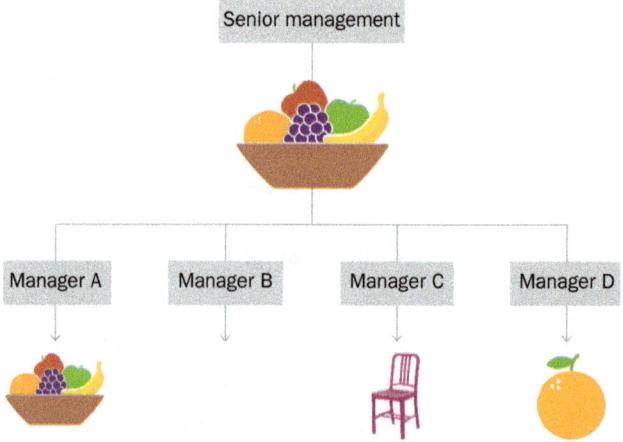

Figure 5. The problem with cascade communication.

The model reflects a classic situation where senior management has communicated a message (the fruit basket), which is to be communicated to the organization. Some managers choose to be loyal to the whole message and convey it identically to employees. Others take out the fruit that they deem relevant and ignore the rest. Some have misunderstood the message and end up conveying a very different picture. And finally, there are those who choose not to communicate.

If it's the wish of senior management that the message should be cascaded down in the organization, perfectly uniform, then Manager A has completed the job satisfactorily. However, there can still be problems if the manager's communication is not adjusted to the target group and is therefore perceived as irrelevant to the next level (employees). At the same time, it's often very clear to employees whether Manager A has truly understood and taken ownership of the message or simply "rattled it off".

Manager B, who chooses not to communicate, may not have been aware that this was expected. Senior management has not been efficient enough in saying that there was a communication task embedded in the communication. Another explanation may be that Manager B didn't find the message relevant to the employees. Finally, one explanation could be that Manager B can't vouch for the message and therefore choose not to communicate it.

Manager C has misunderstood the message, which creates noise further down the organization when employees become confused about which message is correct. This can lead to much speculation and concerns from employees and have fatal consequences for employees' trust in the manager.

Manager D has selected individual messages that the manager considers relevant to their target group. The pitfall may be that employees lack the large framework that the selected messages must be interpreted within. Questions like "Why does it make sense?" And "How do we contribute to the strategy?" may arise.

In cascade communication, senior management has a very important communication task for managers. It's the responsibility of senior management to communicate the message to managers, who in turn should adjust the message and make it relevant to the individual employee. In other words, the manager must do what communication theory refers to as "relevance communication".

Relevance communication

Relevance communication is an essential prerequisite to succeed with cascade communication (see the first element: "Target group" in the Leadership Communication Tool Kit, Chapter 9, page 104). If, as a manager, you fail to make your messages relevant to your employees, the manager may be left with a feeling that it's impossible to get through.

The problem may occur if the manager wants to convey a message that is relevant to employees seen from the manager's perspective, but employees find it irrelevant.

The following example is an interview with three employees. They talk about the relevance of their CEO's weekly video blog where he reflects on the past week from an overall strategic level:

A: Yes, I think it's a great idea that he informs us of what's happening, that's ok, but it's rarely anything that affects us.
[…]
Interviewer: So, it's the relevance that's not so …
A: Well, but, I try to listen to it every time, and it's interesting to know that now we will now have 10,000 new customers. It's something like that.
[…]
B: So, it's, yes. And, and when it only takes a minute, so, yes. But I haven't yet, I don't think I've heard a blog yet that has concerned, uh, us.
B: Day-to-day, uh. I think it's a fine way to do it. Just a short, uh, briefing, uh. I don't do it every day; I simply forget it.
[…]
B: Well, I also think it's ok, and I also think it's good to know what's going on and things like that, don't you? But it's not something I, um … Well, I should really think about what it was … what on earth it was he said?
C: Yes.

B: So afterwards, right. Because then you have the focus on your own, right? (Interview with works managers 2016)

Here it's relevance that becomes the focal point for employees' assessment of the blog. As a starting point, employees would like to be informed about the major strategic picture of the organization, but at the same time, they find it difficult to relate to it and get it prioritized as their main focus is on their own work duties.

In communication theory, this is called "conflicting relevance" (Becker-Jensen 2001), which means that there is a discrepancy between the sender and recipient relevance.

Sender relevance describes the sender's assessment of the message as relevant to the recipient, while recipient relevance refers to what the recipient believes has relevance. When the employee says: "I don't think I've heard a blog yet that has concerned, uh, us", so it just shows that what is close is considered relevant. That may conflict with senior management's relevance assessment where the priority is that all employees should have insight into the organization's strategic direction. When, as in this example, the discrepancy is between the sender and recipient relevance, we can talk about conflicting relevance.

There may also be situations where some messages have different consequences for different target groups. At a meeting for all concerned at Domea.dk where a new strategy was launched, there was subsequent speculation among employees about the messages. The employees found themselves on very different organizational levels, while at the same time they were affected very differently by the strategy. Some employees saw the digitization track as irrelevant in relation to their job functions, while others speculated on whether the new app would mean redundancies. As the message in this way has different meanings for different recipients, it's called "divergent recipient relevance" as it's among the recipients the relevance is different, and not between the sender and recipient.

If the sender and recipient agree that a message has relevance to the recipient, it's a case of "mutual relevance". Mutual relevance is a prerequisite that employees take the message to heart. Therefore, middle managers have a huge task in getting strategic messages to have relevance for the individual employee. This task has been described as the "What's in it for me task".

Middle manager's communication task is complicated

The complexity of getting employees to acquire knowledge means that in many ways, middle managers have a more demanding communication task than senior management. Where senior management's job is primarily about communicating the major strategic picture, the middle manager is standing in the goal and accounting for senior management's strategic messages. The middle manager must be able to *both* put the messages into their own context *and* convey relevance. In other words, the middle manager must be able to explain the impact of the strategic decisions on the department, team and individual.

This interpretation task requires that managers have a profound insight into the organization's strategy and goals (Bordum 2016). The more middle managers have been involved in the strategy process, the easier it is for them to achieve this deep understanding of the strategy, which enables them to communicate it to employees.

Middle managers' challenges are often rooted in fear of not having enough insight and understanding of the strategic messages, as middle managers in many cases have not helped to make the decisions or devise the strategy. This situation may explain why Manager B chooses not to communicate.

The analysis report *Study of strategy work in Danish companies* (Holmgren and Friis 2014) shows that involvement is a development point for many organizations. The report is based on a major study conducted in 2013 when 725 respondents from 140 companies answered questions about Danish companies' way of working with strategy. There are three results that are particularly interesting in the report, seen from a communication perspective:

1. *There is a strong consensus among senior management, middle managers and employees that senior management is involved* in the development of the corporate strategy.

2. *Middle managers' level of involvement is lower than senior management's and employees' perception of how involved they are.* Employees, in particular, have a perception that middle managers are more involved than they themselves perceive it.
3. *The employees' level of involvement is very low.* The report shows that senior management more than middle managers and employees believe that employees are involved.

On the basis of the report's latter findings, Holmgren and Friis concluded that "[in] view of how important it can be for a strategy's successful implementation that employees support and are motivated to make it happen, there is an area here for companies to work with" (ibid.: 8). Seen from a leadership communication perspective, the report shows that there is great potential in increasing the involvement of middle managers.

In addition to the lack of involvement, it's also vital to remember that senior management has typically had slightly more time to consider and digest strategic messages. The following model shows the difference in time there can be with regards to relating to the content:

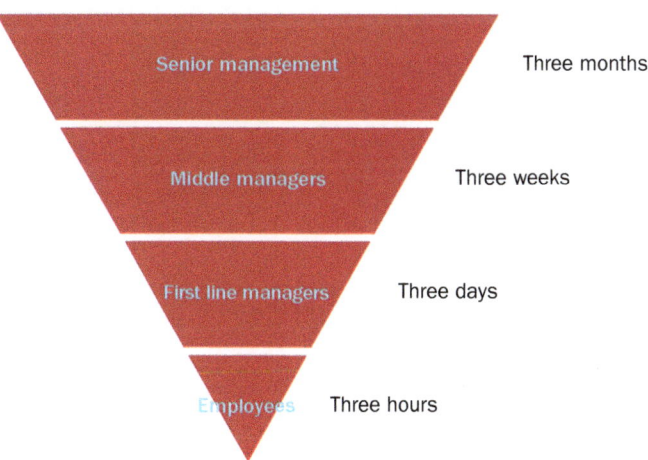

Figure 6. Time model.

Where senior management has worked with the new initiatives for three months, they may choose to involve middle managers three weeks before first line managers, who in turn have a three-day head start on employees who might have a three-hour review of the decision at a meeting for all concerned.

Not surprisingly, it can be a massive challenge for middle and first line managers to succeed in the communication under these conditions. This is problematic because employees have a need to understand the organization's messages, so they don't feel disconnected. As mentioned earlier, leadership communication revolves around three communication paradigms: information, communication and involvement. It's apparent that the further down in the time model we get, the more it's a case of pure information from management to employees, rather than the more involved communication. As the next chapter shows, there are limits to what you as a manager can achieve with information.

Chapter 4
Leadership communication's three forms of communication

As we mentioned in the book's opening chapters, the form of communication is chosen based on the *purpose* of the communication (communication objective).

Already in the definition of "leadership communication" (see page 37), we can identify various communication objectives:

> Leadership communication should be understood as a task to provide employees with *information* about day-to-day activities and facilitate activities and/or *promote understanding and ownership* of the organization's strategy.

To inform, promote understanding and ownership are examples of different purposes the sender may have with their communication. The purpose should form the basis of the way you as a manager choose to convey your message. If the purpose is to educate and inform employees, then it may be sufficient to transmit the message with one-way communication. If the purpose is to engage and get a connection to the message, a dialogue-based approach is necessary.

However, it can be a challenge in practice to make a sharp distinction between what you can achieve with which forms of communication. If, as a manager, you have managed to create a good communication environment, you can achieve a high degree of connectivity just through an e-mail or other relatively limited channels. However, this requires that over a long time, you have built up a communication environment in which feedback from employees has been appreciated. At the same time, the manager's credibility – or what we in Chapter 1 called "ethos" – is crucial. If the sender is seen as trustworthy from the recipient's eyes, you can base your message on trust.

It should also be mentioned that different organizational cultures and management styles also play a crucial role in the forms of communication that work in a specific context. However, in this chapter, we will take our starting point in the characteristics that are typically associated with the various communication objectives and forms.

The potential of leadership communication

Leadership communication offers greater potential than merely informing. The potential to create ownership, commitment, dedication or change behaviour is the reason why leadership communication has become an important management tool, especially in connection with change projects. These different objectives can be placed on an axis, where knowledge represents one extreme and employees' ownership on the other extreme:

| Knowledge | Have an opinion | Change behaviour | Take ownership |

Figure 7. Communication objectives. Source: Inspired by Nielsen 2010a.

It's essential to be aware that the model's various communication objectives require different forms of communication. Getting employees to take ownership or change behaviour requires other forms of communication than it does if you just want to inform employees about a plan or decision. Here it's a prerequisite that the manager is also able to get *involved and create meaning together with the employees*. It should be mentioned that dialogue is not always enough to get people to change their behaviour, and therefore it may be necessary that communication is followed up by objectives, changes of practice and/or skills development.

Being aware that leadership communication may deal with all three forms of communication (transmission, dialogue and involvement), *is important in relation to succeeding in your communication.* The three forms of communication all have legitimacy in leadership communication. One form of communication is not "better" than another. The point is that the choice of the form of communication must be made based on what you want to achieve with your communication. Leadership communication's three forms of communication should be read in conjunction with the communication objectives.

The model below shows which forms of communication have the potential to achieve the various communication objectives (in Chapters 9 and 11 there are examples of how to work with the various forms and objectives of communication in practice):

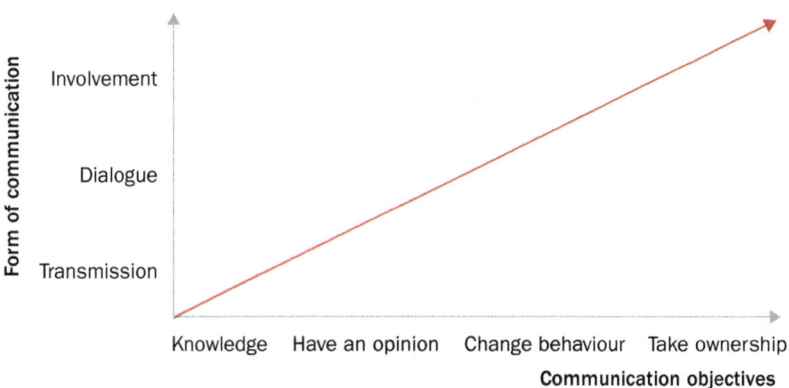

Figure 8. Form of communication and communication objectives.

A series of questions can be linked to each form of communication that show what the purpose is of that communication. Has the manager focused on whether the recipient has *received* and *understood* the message? Or is the manager interested in *how* employees have understood the message? It can also be added to what extent the message in each form of communication is formulated prior to the communication or if it's created in the situation:

	Form of communication	Questions	Message
1	Transmission: Information from the manager to employees	Did you receive my message?	The message is formulated in advance of the communication
2	Dialogue: Communication between the manager and employees	Did you understand my message?	
3	Involvement: Involving employees	How do you understand/interpret my message?	The message is created in the communication situation in collaboration between the manager and employees

Figure 9. Form of communication, question and message.

It's quite key for communication whether the message is formulated in advance of the communication or whether it's created in the communication situation. The traditional way of thinking about leadership communication is often based on a form of control, as we saw with cascade communication in the previous chapter. Here senior management has "control" of the message as it's typically prepared in advance before the rest of the organization are involved. On the other hand, if the message is established jointly between employees and management, it's crucial that you as a manager can relinquish some of the control and be open to employees' understanding. In this situation, there is a movement towards another way of thinking about leadership communication. This can be illustrated by coupling the three forms of communication with three different communication paradigms.

Leadership communication's three forms and paradigms

The first form of communication, "transmission", is based on information transmitted *from* the sender to recipient and is part of the "information paradigm". The question "Did you receive my message?" indicates that there is a communication situation where the manager prior to the conversation has formed a message that employees must be aware of. It could possibly be decisions that employees just need to be informed about. The information paradigm doesn't account for the recipient's pre-understanding and its impact on the interpretation of the message. This means that the manager doesn't ask about employees' understanding of and opinion of the decision but is more concerned with whether the employees have received the information.

The other form of communication, "dialogue", is based on communication *between* management and employees and therefore falls under what is called the "communication paradigm". Unlike the information paradigm, it's dialogue-based, as it has the interaction, i.e., the dialogue, as the focal point. Here the manager, in the same way, has formed a message prior to the conversation, but here the employee must not only be aware of this message but also understand it. The question "Have you understood my message?" is the focal point of the "dialogue" form of communication. This question can lead to a dialogue between the manager and employees, leading to a common understanding, for example, of the rationale behind a strategic decision.

The last form of communication, "involvement", falls under what goes by the name of the "involvement paradigm". This paradigm is based on the manager involving employees and creating an interpretive framework in which employees can create meaning and interpretation in interaction with each other and the manager. Here no specific message is created prior to communication. The message is instead created in the communication situation in a collaboration (read more about how messages are formed in the Leadership Communication Tool Kit in Chapter 9). The involvement paradigm is just like the communication paradigm, dialogic, but the focal point is "*How* do you understand/interpret my message?".

	Form of communication	Questions	Message	Communication paradigm
1	*Transmission:* Information from the manager to employees	Did you receive my message?	The message is formulated in advance of the communication	The information paradigm
2	*Dialogue:* Communication between the manager and employees	Did you understand my message?		The communication paradigm
3	*Involvement:* Involving employees	How do you understand/interpret my message?	The message is created in the communication situation in collaboration between the manager and employees	The involvement paradigm

Figure 10. Form of communication, question, message and communication paradigm.

The three forms of communication, questions, messages and associated paradigms will be discussed in the following chapters to show how leadership communication can be built upon each paradigm, as well as the potential and limitations each one has. The purpose of the chapters is to raise awareness of the opportunities and limitations associated with each of the three communication paradigms, so the manager is in a better position to make an informed choice in relation to which form of communication is most appropriate to use to meet the communication objective.

Chapter 5
Leadership communication as information

Many senior managers consider the job of communication as a matter of sending or transmitting information to the organization (Zerfass and Sherzada 2015). This perception of communication falls under the information paradigm and typically involves information from the manager to employees.

The term "balcony speech" used in some organizations to describe this kind of one-way communication, illustrates the mindset quite well.

Figure 11. Speech from the balcony of the Court of Roskilde. Photo: Bjørn Armbjørn.

In a communication context, the word "balcony speech" is often negative as it's the image of manager's transmission-orientated approach to the job of communication: to communicate a message to as many employees as possible through one-way communication. The message is defined in advance, so the task is to get employees to become aware of the message.

The advantage of this type of communication is that all employees receive the same message at the same time. Many managers see this as an advantage, as rumours don't spread in the organization, as is often the case when communication takes place in dribs and drabs. Senior management may particularly benefit from this form of communication since it's precisely their job to communicate the big picture.

Middle managers are then left with the local communication in their respective team and stand, so to speak, in the line of fire in relation to senior management's communication. Here it's crucial that middle managers are equipped for this interpretation task; through a dialogue-based communication with senior management, and that they have some communication material to use as a base. It's also important that senior management stick to the big picture and don't encroach on middle managers' management options.

Did you receive my message?

Whether the sender succeeds with this form of communication is clarified by asking the recipient group the following question: Did you receive my message? The question can be formulated in different ways: Did you get the e-mail I sent yesterday? Did you participate in the meeting the other day? Have you seen the PowerPoint presentation? The tools can be e-mails, newsletters, flyers, information, magazines, news on the intranet, video communication, etc.

With online media, we are able to make qualitative studies, where you can track how many people have visited a website or clicked on a piece of news. So, you can measure how many employees actually received (but not necessarily understood!) the message.

The information paradigm's communication understanding

One-way communication is based on what is known as a *functionalist* basic understanding of communication. Communication here is about distributing information "effectively". Communication is seen as something an organization *has* on an equal footing with other management tools, and which takes place *inside* organizations: Some tell, explain or convey messages. The organization is seen as a container in which communication takes place – in a more or less effective manner (Ashcraft et al. 2009: 19).

The perception of communication as a linear process, emanating from the sender and transmitted to the recipient is reflected, for example, in a job advertisement where an organization was looking for a chief adviser for internal communication, who would "ensure relevant and professional internal communication from management on strategic matters". This form of leadership communication will often be about communication channels, i.e., how the organization's message reaches as many employees as possible. Initiatives such as the preparation of newsletters or higher frequency of news on the intranet will be in focus, especially because the goal is typically to give employees *sufficient* information. The purpose is also in accordance with the form of communication in the paradigm that this chapter is about, the *information paradigm*. Through transmission, the manager can inform their employees about a given message.

The form of communication, transmission, is also known as "needle theory" as the form of communication is characterized by a perception that the messages are almost injected into the recipient, regardless of what is communicated. The sender normally has focus on their message but has less interest in whether the recipient actually understands the message. The sender sees it as their job to get the message delivered or transmitted to the recipient. This affects the way the message is communicated.

When the message is formulated in advance of the communication

When managers stand up on the soapbox and transmit a strategic message to the organization, the language often contains arguments. This means that employees receive messages through an argumentative form of communication: The manager conveys their message by formulating a need ("We must focus on the customer") backed by a premise ("It's one of our core values"). Understandably, this argument is based on consensus in the organization that when you say that you are customer-orientated, then you must also be customer-orientated ("You have to act on your values").

It's essential that the sender and recipient agree on the premise. Otherwise, the recipient won't accept the argument or perceive it as bad. The premise of an organization will be, for example, values. It could be a strategic value of being customer-orientated. However, it's rare that you start your argument by referring to such a premise, as it's supposed to be a foregone conclusion. In rhetoric, this form of indirect communication is called "enthymeme". If the form of communication is to succeed, it's essential that the employees and the manager share the same organizational values and identity. If not, we can misunderstand each other.

Employee satisfaction survey: Have you been informed?

That communication is regarded as a matter of channelling messages to the organization is also reflected in the very comprehensive employee satisfaction surveys, which many companies and organizations use. Traditional formulations in such surveys where employees are asked for their assessment, might be "I feel well-informed about what is happening in the organization", "My immediate manager has clearly explained how I am expected to contribute, so my team achieves our goals" or "My immediate manager clearly informs me about the direction and goals for my team". The formulations are based on whether the sender (i.e., the manager) has distributed enough information, which reflects the underlying information paradigm in which the recipient remains a passive entity in the communication situation. This approach to leadership communication often gives rise to an opinion among employees that it's the manager's job to make sure that employees feel sufficiently informed, which can also be supported by a lack of expectations in relation to "how we communicate in this company". This can create a culture where employees are never satisfied with communication, and they feel either over- or under-informed.

The legitimacy of the information paradigm

This does not mean that the transmission of messages across the organization without further dialogue is not worth considering. Practical information can be sent out without problems to the organization via a common e-mail, a notice in the canteen or other channels that don't necessarily invite dialogue (read more about selecting a channel in the Leadership Communication Tool Kit in Chapter 9).

The following e-mail that was sent to all employees at the University of Southern Denmark (SDU) is an example of how the sender transmits their message to the target group:

 Remember your access card/personnel card after 5 p.m. and during the weekend

> Hello Everybody,
> A reminder that you need to remember your access card/personnel card when you leave your office after 5 p.m. and during the weekend. The sliding glass doors on the 4th and 5th floors and the lifts and stair towers automatically lock during these periods, and therefore you will need to use your card (and password) to get into the locked areas.

When it comes to practical information, as shown in this example, it's about *informing*. If it turns out that employees don't follow the stated guidelines, you may later consider informing them in a more interesting way to capture your target group, and in a way that's easier to remember and relate to.

An example of how to capture your target group with one-way communication is the University of Southern Denmark's information campaign on their state of emergency. The university has produced a short film that shows where to find safety information, and what to do in an emergency situation. The target group is students, teachers and other guests.

Figure 12. Emergency contingency film for the University of Southern Denmark's information campaign.

In the film, a flight attendant guides the recipient through the various procedures. A figure is in the background performs the various operational instructions. The film uses humour, and it creates awareness, partly because of the contrast with the film's serious message about the action required with regard to a potential state of emergency. The aim of the film, according to the University of Southern Denmark, is to present "the most important thing about the emergency contingency that you need to relate to and be informed of" (SDU 2016).

The film is a supplement to the following notices that are found in all rooms:

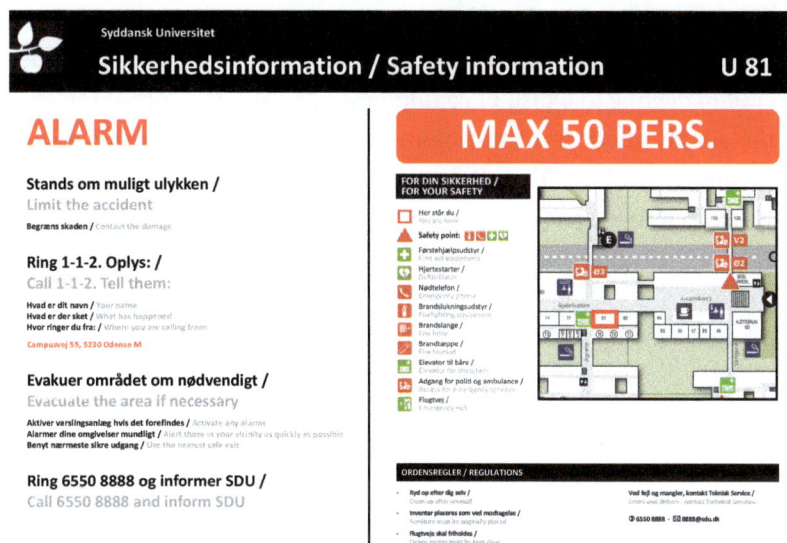

Figure 13. Safety information displayed at the University of Southern Denmark.

The example shows that despite one-way communication, it's possible through various means and media to personify the message and create an emotional response in the recipient (amusement) that makes an impression.

Limitations of the information paradigm

One-way communication typically serves to inform and orientate the recipient about a given subject, but it's limited in terms of changing the recipient's opinion or behaviour. Therefore, there must be very effective one-way communication before it can influence the opinions and behaviour of the recipient. An example of weak one-way communication are the photos on cigarette packs showing various diseases. Although the photos show the fatal consequences of smoking, studies have shown that they don't dissuade smokers from lighting their next cigarette.

If the purpose of the communication is to *change* the recipient's opinion or behaviour, it's, therefore, necessary to supplement with more dialogue-based channels. The task then changes character from a question of *informing* to a task of *communicating*. Here the communication is not simply about transmitting messages, but rather to reach a common understanding. This dialogue-based form of communication is also referred to as the "communication paradigm".

Chapter 6
Leadership communication as communication

Communication *between* management and employees is about moving from the information paradigm and the idea of passing on a message, to a dialogic approach to communication, where the sender and recipient achieve a common understanding of what the message means. However, this is often embedded in the fact that it's the employees who must understand the management's message, as the manager has the power and holds the truth. So, there is a case of dialogic communication where the manager and employees have a dialogue – or interaction – about the already defined message. This interaction gives its name to the paradigm we now will look at; the *communication paradigm*.

Did you understand my message?

In the communication paradigm, the key issue changes from acting on whether employees have *received* the message, to a question of whether employees have *understood* the message. Common to both the information paradigm and the communication paradigm is that prior to communication, some messages are prepared that the recipient will receive (the information paradigm) or understand (the communication paradigm). When it comes to achieving a common understanding, it's actually a matter of the employees understanding the manager's message. Whether or not the sender has succeeded with this aim can be clarified by asking the employee the following question: Did you understand my message? This can then lead to further questions such as: Is there anything that is unclear to you? Do you have any questions about the material? Is there anything you are unsure about?

The communication paradigm's communication understanding

Where the information paradigm is based on a functionalist basic understanding of communication, the communication paradigm is linked to the *constitutionalist* basic view where communication is considered as what constitutes or creates the organization (see Aggerholm et al. (2010) for a thorough examination of the two basic views). The constitutional approach came into focus around the turn of the millennium (Craig 1999; McPhee and Zaug 2000) and has subsequently been the domain for a variety of research publications. The container as a metaphor has been replaced by the concept of "equivalence" (i.e. having the same value), and the communication is equated with the organization. The mutual relationship between communication and the organization means that we are dealing with dimensions that are up for constant negotiation.

The communication paradigm has, amongst other things, materialized in terms such as "top-down" and "bottom-up communication". It signals that there is not exclusive focus on communication from management to employees, but also communication from employees to management. In practice, this has meant that HR departments are often involved in facilitating processes for managers. Employees have become accustomed to being invited to workshops where everyone can have their say and be heard.

Awareness of the communication paradigm is also present in the job advertisement we mentioned in Chapter 5, where it's expected that the future chief adviser "plans and assists in information and dialogue meetings, and continuously develops the internal dialogue culture" (page 61). When the organization makes a distinction between information meetings and dialogue meetings, it undoubtedly reflects a deliberate use of the information and communication paradigms, as well as recognition that they often coexist.

Employee satisfaction survey: just an indication?

That the purpose of communication is to get employees to understand a predefined message is reflected in the typical statements employees are asked to consider in connection with employee satisfaction surveys. Here are some examples: "I understand the company's overall goals", "I have a clear understanding of the department's goals" and "I can see how I contribute to the organization's overall performance". The purpose of the questions is to determine whether the employee has a sense of having understood the messages that management has communicated. However, they don't uncover whether this is indeed the case.

The problem with such types of questions is that management does not get insight into *how* the employee has interpreted the message or the employee's *opinion* of the message. Therefore, the subjective interpretation process is not taken into account, which we reviewed in Chapter 3, and neither that we interpret messages based on our own preconceptions. So what can you as a manager use the answers to these questions for? Well, not much else than to get a sense of whether the employees themselves feel that they have understood the strategic messages. To what extent these are interpreted appropriately or not can't be concluded from the questions. A qualitative approach is needed here such as employee interviews, where you can ask about *how* the employee interprets the messages.

The legitimacy of the communication paradigm

That employees understand a predefined message has its legitimacy in communication situations where the message is not up for discussion. The dialogue in this paradigm is explanatory and is intended to sufficiently equip employees to act as desired.

An example of a dialogue-based meeting format that many senior managers have used in recent years is the so-called "town hall meetings" or "soapbox meetings" where senior management invites all employees to a meeting. "Standing on a soapbox" has been one way for senior management to talk about the organization's overall objectives and status while creating space for dialogue. Town hall meetings are often used to launch a major communication in an organization when there must be a change. As a starting point, the meeting must be followed up by the line manager's communication (cascade communication), so the overall messages are relevant for each department (see the section on relevance communication in Chapter 3) and are therefore not merely transmitted.

Limitations of the communication paradigm

It's our experience that many resources are used to strengthen dialogue within organizations. In addition to town hall meetings and cascade communication, other initiatives can be mentioned that are gaining ground, such as "coffee meetings" where managers engage in dialogue with people several levels below themselves. This led Kevin Ruck to question whether the growing criticism of internal communication focusing primarily on communications from management to employees is at all legitimate (Ruck 2015: 52).

If we look towards practice, it turns out, however, that many organizations worldwide are still experiencing major communication challenges in spite of their increased efforts in terms of integrating the communication paradigm and its focus on both the sender and recipient.

The problem can be illustrated by looking at the cascade concept as a metaphor. If you look up "cascade" in the Cambridge English Dictionary, it's described as "to fall quickly and in large amounts". However, that is seldom the experience employees are left with when messages are cascaded into the organization. On the contrary, the problem – as described in Chapter 3 – is that the cascade stops before it really gets going.

Another challenge with cascade communication is that senior management, from where the cascade typically originates, don't take their starting point in the needs of the recipients of the messages but rather take their starting point in their own need to inform (see the section on relevance communication in Chapter 3). Or maybe middle managers don't agree with senior management's decision, and so they merely settle for passing on senior management's decision without adjusting the communication to the target group. This can create a culture where cascading simply becomes a matter of forwarding the information, and so communication rests on the information paradigm. The effect of this way of thinking about communication is most often measured by employee surveys, which don't measure employees' real understanding.

Finally, it's vital that management understands that an invitation for dialogue is just an invitation. Although the form of communication encourages dialogue, it doesn't mean that employees accept the invitation. That a dialogue-based form of communication doesn't necessarily translate into dialogue, is an experience that many managers have had themselves. For example, in connection with an oral presentation in the form of a town hall or soapbox meeting where the manager then encourages employees to ask questions but is met with a wall of silence. Here constructive questions like "Who has the first question?" fail. Or perhaps the post box, where employees can ask questions which management will answer at the next meeting, remains empty week after week. This apparent rejection of dialogue is in stark contrast to the recommendations of the many researchers and theorists who consider face-to-face communication as the richest form of communication, as it allows for immediate feedback, verbal and non-verbal communication, interaction and determination with respect to a specific recipient (Daft and Lengel 1986). As Kjærbeck and Lundholt (2018b) have shown, there is a tendency that management helps to obstruct dialogue by, for instance, not going into the details of the criticisms that employees raise or by responding to specific problems with abstract strategic objectives like "We want to be the front-runner", "We are ambitious" or "We set the bar high".

The rejection of dialogue can also derive from employees perceiving that the purpose of the meeting is to transmit information, even though the manager hopes to have a dialogue with the employees. It's important to recognize that you, as a manager, must be aware of what you can expect to get out of a meeting. If the purpose of the meeting is to inform the employees, it's certainly a proper and realistic purpose. However, if the original goal was also to engage in dialogue with the employees, then we have to find other forms of meetings to supplement with and so to recognize that town hall or soapbox meetings are not suitable for dialogue.

Asymmetrical relationship

A vital issue that can keep employees from engaging in dialogue may be the presence of an asymmetrical relationship between the communicating parties, i.e., the unequal power relationship that inherently exists between managers and employees. This can create a fear of "asking stupid questions".

The unequal power relationship can help to slow down initiatives for dialogue. Here it's important to remember that the opposite of asymmetrical communication, i.e., symmetrical communication, doesn't in itself create a good dialogue. Here an open communication environment is an essential prerequisite. We will return to this in Chapter 8.

Another critical point came to light in an interview with the Executive Management of a large Danish company. The CFO explained here that if senior management is to succeed with communication, the management style of middle managers is crucial:

> So, the places where there is such an elitist culture in which the middle manager decides everything, knows everything and is almost god personified, right [...] it's clear that it's extremely difficult to get a dialogue going because they [the employees] sit there and are in fact afraid of getting a rap over the knuckles. And the places where you have some modern middle managers, who encourage dialogue and so on, [...] it's much easier. (Interview with Executive Management 2016)

The CFO described how the relationship between direct management and employees plays a role in relation to how much dialogue occurs at a soapbox meeting. He supplemented with the following observation: "They sit there and look at their boss, before deciding what kind of facial expressions and gestures they may have". In such situations, there is also an asymmetrical relationship, but here it's the middle manager and not senior management who have power over employees.

Although there will always be a power difference between the organizational levels, you can as a manager use various processes to create an equal communication. The power relationship can, for example, get a more retracted role if messages are created together with the employees, instead of the communication situation being based on the manager having previously formulated a message that employees must understand. Then there is namely a case of an involvement process, and it's the foundation of the third paradigm: the *involvement paradigm* that we will look at in Chapter 7.

Chapter 7
Leadership communication as involvement

The following quote illustrates the essence of what management's job is when you want to achieve employee ownership:

> If you want to build a ship, don't drum up people to collect wood and don't assign them tasks and work, but rather teach them to long for the endless immensity of the sea. (de Saint-Exupéry 1943)

Hart and Quinn (1993) have given this role the name of "vision setter", and it's about creating a sense of identity and mission. Westley and Minzberg (1989) describe the vision setters as those who can "translate" the vision to employees across different media through words, as well as action (also quoted in Argenti 2017). However, there is an embedded perception in this that the translation task, i.e., the interpretation of the strategy, is exclusively placed with management and that the employees are reduced to objects that are "exposed" to the vision. Since the key to commitment and ownership is that employees have the option to interpret meaning into the strategic messages, it's not sufficient to expose them to the visions and messages. On the contrary, employees must be able to interpret strategic messages from their own subjective horizons of understanding and interaction with others. This requires that you as a manager are able to involve employees, allowing them to create their own interpretations based on the dialogue with the manager and other colleagues.

When you talk about communication as involving, then you place yourself within the third communication paradigm: *the involvement paradigm*. As mentioned, the involvement paradigm shares the communication paradigm's dialogical form, but the involvement paradigm differs by focusing on the recipient's *interpretation* rather than understanding the message.

How do you understand the message?

The involvement paradigm is not only to identify and understand the original meaning or importance, but rather to create a new common sense on the basis of past, current and future scenarios. The message is not necessarily a fixed designed dimension, but rather something that can occur in the process. This reflects a central movement from the information paradigm's focus on getting the message transmitted, to the communication paradigm's focus on whether the recipient has understood the message, and over to the involvement paradigm, which focuses on the importance the recipient attributes to the message in the interpretation process.

The involvement paradigm's communication understanding

In addition to embracing the two-way communication and dialogue between the communicating parties, the constitutionalist basic view takes communication a step further and focuses on how the message is interpreted by the recipient and the associated formation of meaning.

The essence of working with the involvement paradigm is to recognize that contrary to the information and communication paradigm, the message is not necessarily a fixed designed dimension, which is developed prior to the communication situation, but rather something that can occur in the process.

The involvement paradigm is not only to identify and understand the original meaning or significance of a message but to create a new common meaning on the basis of past, current and future scenarios. This reflects a central movement from the information paradigm's focus on getting the message transmitted, to the communication paradigm's focus on whether the recipient has understood the message, and over to the involvement paradigm, which focuses on the importance the recipient attributes to the message in the interpretation process.

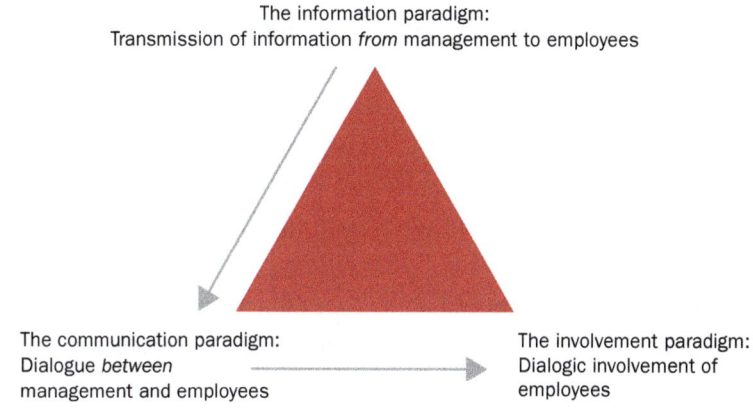

Figure 14. The three communication paradigms.

The movement from the information paradigm over to the communication paradigm and on to the involvement paradigm should not be understood in the way that information and communication paradigms are to be replaced by the involvement paradigm. It's more a matter of being able to use all three paradigms in leadership communication.

When we work with the involvement paradigm, we focus on involving employees in *creating* messages.

When the message is formulated in the communication situation

When the message has to be formulated as an interaction between the manager and employees, it's necessary that the manager invites reflection. Then the production domain should be replaced with the reflection domain (see Chapter 1). In contrast to the production domain, here, as mentioned, there is not one strictly defined truth, but many truths. The objective of communication doesn't revolve around getting employees to understand one particular message, but rather to invite a dialogue with the aim to interpret and formulate messages jointly.

To create involvement, it's important that you as a manager are ready to share the communication responsibility with your employees. When communication is developed in the interaction between the manager and employees, both parties have a responsibility for the outcome. At the same time, the manager must have the courage to relinquish control of the communication situation, which can be transgressive, as the manager's usual form of communication is argumentative and is based on a message that exists prior to the communication.

In addition to partially relinquishing responsibility, the manager must "park" the arguments and make room for reflection. Reflection is achieved when employees are willing to share points of views and opinions with colleagues and the manager to reach a common understanding. Reflection can obviously not be imposed on employees. It requires that the manager abandons the logos appeal form and makes room for a more ethos and pathos orientated communication.

Ethos is a prerequisite for involvement communication, as this form of dialogue is based on the relationship of trust that exists between managers and employees. If employees have confidence in the manager, there is a greater willingness to contribute to a common understanding. If the trust relationship doesn't exist or has suffered a serious blow, it can be very difficult for the manager to invite open dialogue and reflection. The relationship must be built up again.

In the involvement paradigm, the employees' interpretation of the message is the focal point. When an interpretation is an internal process, the path to this form of communication can be found through pathos and more emotional language. Verbs like "sense", "think", "understand", "interpret" and "feel" give access to the employees' own interpretations of the messages. At the same time, the emotional language can open up for an inner connection to the messages, which the rational, logos-orientated form of communication doesn't achieve to the same degree.

To access employees' many reflections and interpretations, it's also crucial that as a manager you create a framework for dialogue that supports the involvement element. Here, as a manager, you can usefully take inspiration from the following ten points of inspiration:

1. Be value-neutral.
2. Accept feedback and criticism.
3. Listen rather than convince.
4. Accept different worldviews.
5. Be curious.
6. Be investigative.
7. Be concerned with understanding what the other person understands.
8. Show sincere interest in the other person and their concerns.
9. Focus on employees' relationship to change.
10. Listen for the unsaid.

It may be supplemented with six points of awareness, which the manager must refrain from in the communication situation:

1. Controlling.
2. Concluding.
3. Focused on right and wrong.
4. Reproachful.
5. Impatient.
6. Stubborn.
    (Prepared by Dalager and Lundholt 2017)

As mentioned, it may be a challenge for managers to act within the involvement form of communication as it can be quite unfamiliar. A prerequisite to switching between the different domains is the knowledge that you as a manager can achieve various objectives with your leadership communication, depending on which form of communication you allow to be the framework for communication.

Employee satisfaction survey: Does it make sense?

Since communication is perceived as a process of interpretation, it challenges the understanding of the manager's responsibility, whether it succeeds or not. When communication occurs in the interaction between the manager and employees, and at the same time depends on both internal and external factors of the individual employee, which the manager has no influence over, the burden of whether communication is successful isn't solely attributed to the manager; rather, it must be attributed to both parties. If you have to examine satisfaction in relation to communication within an organization, it must, therefore, complement traditional questions like "Do you feel informed?" with more interpretive questions such as "How do the messages make sense to you in relation to your daily work?".

If we return to employee satisfaction measurements, we often only find a limited number of statements that contain an interpretive element. An example is: "My duties and job content are meaningful to me".

The most optimal way to collect information about employees' interpretation of strategic messages is to complement the quantitative measurement with qualitative surveys, where through an interview you ask about how employees interpret strategic messages.

The legitimacy of the involvement paradigm

Since the involvement paradigm is primarily characterized by the message being established in collaboration between the manager and employees, the messages must have some flexibility before it makes sense to involve employees. It could be overall strategic messages that have not yet been translated into action. This would create great value if the employees were given an opportunity to reflect on how they interpret the strategic directions within their area. Conversely, the open space for interpretation will not be present in the context of a round of redundancies in which messages are clearly defined from the start. However, in connection with follow-up communication among both permanent and laid-off employees, where communication is intended to give employees the opportunity to reflect on the consequences of these changes, the involvement paradigm would come into its own.

However, a prerequisite is that the manager establishes some interpretation frameworks, so the interpretation doesn't end up with unintended conclusions. If management fails to establish an appropriate framework of understanding (see the example on page 43 regarding clarification of the consultant's role), it causes more speculation, and it may eventually affect both employee satisfaction and productivity in general. In other words, the interpretation process is left to employees who seek to make sense on their own, which can lead to incorrect conclusions.

The frustration that occurs in extension of this is not a question of whether you, in this example, have a management team who resist change. Rather than talking about resistance to change, you could talk about resistance towards a lack of meaning (Dent and Goldberg 1999; Bordum 2016).

Resistance towards a lack of meaning?

To talk of "resistance towards a lack of meaning" rather than "resistance to change" is an alternative way to attack the problem. Firstly, it moves part of the focus away from the employees as the main problem in the change process, as *involving employees and creating meaning in interaction is not only the employee's responsibility but a joint task between the manager and employees.* When we talk about leadership communication, it's vital that employees are given the opportunity in interaction with management to interpret strategic messages, so they make sense to them. It's important if the communication objective is to create ownership. It's a slightly more time-consuming process, and some managers claim that they don't have time for that sort of thing. Here it's crucial to remember that it can have a long-term positive effect on the relationship between the manager and employees by involving employees, and similarly, it can have a long-term negative effect *not* to do it. Therefore, it may be a good investment in the long run.

In this light, it makes no sense to speak of "ready for change" and "agile" employees, as these terms indicate that the employee must take on a special role to meet management's needs. What is instead needed is that employees interpret strategic messages. To interpret is quite a natural process for people so that employees are in fact always "ready for interpretation". However, there may be people who oppose because of a lack of agreement or motives. In such cases, it's essential that the manager gets acquainted with what is at stake, and then devise an appropriate strategy for dealing with the situation.

Limitations of the involvement paradigm

The involvement paradigm's greatest limitation is that it doesn't require a fixed defined message. This can obviously lead to employees leaving the meeting or workshop with different interpretations of which direction the company is moving in. Management must manoeuvre in a delicate balance between creating a context that is indicative and guiding relative to the desired direction, while at the same time creating space for employees' interpretation. What matters is that as a manager you create an interpretive framework that employees can process information with and make sense of. It's also an essential condition that the manager has been through an involvement process with their managers, and that the manager has experienced that the messages make sense.

If you consider communication as a constant social process in which meaning is something that occurs continuously, and is not a fixed dimension, it also means that communication is an area that can't easily be controlled by the manager. The message is not a fixed dimension but occurs in the *interaction* between the manager and employees (Ruben and Gigliotti 2016). Leadership communication is to some extent unpredictable and uncontrollable seen from a management perspective. A variety of factors come into play in relation to what message the employees interpret. It may be previous decisions, communication channels or the relationship between the manager and employees. In addition, each employee, as mentioned in Chapter 3, has their own preconceptions, which also play a crucial role in the interpretation of the message. It all contributes to the manager having to adjust their perceptions of and expectations to control communication.

Another limitation with respect to the involvement paradigm may be that not all messages need to create ownership. With some messages, the employees just need to have knowledge of them, and others require merely an understanding. In the case of redundancy, for example, there is also a legal aspect, which means that the manager and middle manager can't be entirely transparent. However, although messages associated with such cuts or layoffs, as a rule, are not open to interpretation, and reasons for the decision are not always transparent, it's still important that employees experience an open dialogue on decisions.

To consider leadership communication as a task in facilitating an involvement process and therefore an interpretation process, doesn't necessarily mean significant changes in relation to the way most senior managers have communicated up until now. However, it can heighten awareness about the division of responsibilities between senior management and middle management, just as it may define the task in the sense that senior management can leave the interpretation part to the remaining levels of the organization. It also calls for new skills from middle managers, who must now be able to involve and create meaning in interaction with employees.

Chapter 8
Leadership communication and communication environment

In the previous chapters, we examined the forms of language that separate the involvement paradigm from the information and communication paradigms. In this chapter, we turn to the communication environment, which is an essential prerequisite for achieving employee ownership.

The organization's communication environment

If the objective of communication is to get employees to take ownership, it's crucial that they have the option to give feedback upward in the organization, which creates an open communication environment. An organization with an open communication environment is characterized by the fact that feedback – especially critical feedback from employees to the manager – is valued by management and makes a difference. The concept of "communication environment" covers the communication culture of the organization and can be used to distinguish between the open communication environment where employees' input is recognized, in contrast to the closed communication environment where employees refrain from expressing their opinions.

The terms "open" and "closed" communication environment are widely used among academics and practitioners, but it has not been sufficiently used in literature when you consider how vital a role the communication environment plays in terms of whether communication works or not.

The literature on leadership communication has primarily aimed at communication *from* the manager *to* employees. The research shows that it can have severe consequences for organizations not to focus on communication from employees to the manager, as the organization might miss valuable input from critical voices.

Consequences of a closed communication environment

It's not difficult to find examples of the fatal consequences of a closed communication environment. Therefore, researchers have identified a strong correlation between the Volkswagen scandal in 2015 and employees' critical lack of feedback to management (Monzani et al. 2016). In fact, the closed communication environment was a key factor in the extent of the scandal. The case concerned the manipulation of emission measurements from at least nine million diesel cars. In the manipulated environmental tests, the vehicles appeared to pollute less than they did. The scandal cost Director Martin Winterkorn his job, and VW had to pay approx. EUR 4 billion in fines, while the price of shares went into free fall.

We can find another example of the drastic consequences of a closed communication environment in the IT industry. A study carried out by the software company VMware among IT departments and employees in the Nordic countries, shows that 34% of IT managers have refrained from informing senior management of a major data breach. Lars-Bo Klausen, Country Manager of VMware Denmark, described the underlying challenge to IT security in a press release as "a communication gap between the company's managers and IT managers". By not informing senior management it can result in lowering the priority of security measures in companies in a time when the threat is serious. The study shows that 76% of IT managers believe that it's likely or very likely that their company will be exposed to a serious attack within the next three months, while only 17% of the companies' other employees share this assessment (Version2 2016).

In addition to resulting in financial difficulties and incorrect decisions, a lack of feedback to management can affect organizational efficiency, innovation, learning and readiness for change and result in unwanted behaviour (Monzani et al. 2016). We see an example in an interview with an employee who became frustrated by his lack of opportunity to pass on his experience and knowledge to management:

> Sometimes I travel around Denmark and find a lot of things, where some of it's excellent, and some of it's terrible [...]. So, they don't all follow the same administrative procedures. But I have then asked, what should we do when we find out that these administrative procedures are incorrect? We need a place where everything is anchored. And so, I stand there and think, "Crikey, and you have travelled to all the service centres and talked about administrative procedures. Now you have found such [...] a large wealth of knowledge that could make it easier for customer service, for all of us". Now I have a wealth knowledge, and then I think, "Uh, what do I do with it now?" [...]. So, how can we move on, because this is actually excellent, it's something that can make everyone's life easier. And somewhere I have the feeling [...] that it's a waste of time that I've travelled around. It's been cosy and very exciting. [...] But now I'm left with a lot of knowledge, and I think, what should I do with it? (Interview with an employee 2016)

The employee at the front line often has an experience of being able to contribute with knowledge and experience that will ultimately improve the established administrative procedures, thus increasing efficiency. However, if employees don't know where and how knowledge can be passed on up in the organization, management misses out on the input that could be of great value. At the same time, employees are perhaps frustrated by not being able to give feedback to management.

Another consequence of criticism that is not communicated is senior management's impression that their opinions are shared by more people than they really are. A lack of responsiveness from senior management – or just employees' perception of a lack of responsiveness – can lead to employees regarding management as untrustworthy (Dundon and Gollan 2007: 1188). Lack of credibility can play a major and negative role when management communicates to employees (see the section on ethos appeal in Chapter 1, page 21). It's crucial here to remember that employees' opportunities to give feedback upward in the organization are the most important and essential mechanism in relation to achieving employee engagement (Truss et al. 2006: 41). If we return to the example of the employee who is left with a feeling that their efforts have been a waste of time, then it's very likely that their engagement has suffered a severe blow.

It's fascinating that the opportunities for employees to give feedback significantly affects their engagement. In a measurement of employee engagement conducted at a large Danish electrical contractor, the survey described "an important element in the decision making when it comes to prioritization of prospective focus areas and to ensure satisfied employees and good management". When employees' opportunity to give feedback is the most important parameter in relation to employee engagement, then it's surprising that the statement "My immediate manager gives me sufficient feedback on my work" is among the 38 statements that employees in this company must assess, whereas statements regarding employees' option to give feedback to the management is not included in the survey. Since the measurement is used as a vital element in the decision making in relation to the focus areas, you could fear that management doesn't have the information needed to make informed decisions.

When silence in relation to organizational issues becomes a collective behaviour among employees, there is what research describes as "organizational silence" (Morrison and Milliken 2000). Researchers have identified various reasons why this phenomenon occurs.

Employee motivation behind organizational silence

Employees' decision not to raise concerns can be explained by both individual and organizational factors. Individual factors may include personality or different kinds of motives, whereas organizational factors may be risk assessment (or outright fear of the consequences), as well as organizational and institutional norms. (is it something "we" just do?). There is general agreement that management can greatly affect whether employees express their opinions or not.

Research shows that managers consciously or unconsciously tend to exhibit behaviour that results in employees refraining from criticizing the organization's strategy or management's behaviour (Tourish and Robson 2006). This behaviour can be expressed as a negative response from management to criticism or even punishing employees who express criticism (for example, less attention, less pay or even dismissal). It can also lead to a culture in which critical employees are considered as misinformed and therefore hushed up (Tourish 1998), or they are perceived as elements that create resistance, which management seeks to eliminate (Lewis 1992). Senior management has a tendency to over-criticize negative feedback, which naturally makes employees refrain from giving criticism going forward (Tourish and Hargie 2004). This reaction pattern helps to create a closed communication environment in which critical feedback doesn't have a natural place.

The following excerpts from an interview about employees' perception of a town hall meeting is an excellent example of how a closed communication environment can be experienced by employees:

> Interviewer: Is senior management well-prepared for these meetings?
> A and B: Yes.
> A: Yes, right to their fingertips.
> Interviewer: Okay, right to their fingertips?
> [...]
> A: Yes, that's for sure.
> B: That's why you must be fully prepared if you have to ask about something or say something, you can't just babble on about anything.
> A: No, you can't do that.
> [...]
> B: You immediately get a pounding. (Interview with caretakers 2016)

Senior management experienced the town hall meetings a lot differently. When they are asked about the purpose of the meetings, the answer is:

> We are of course here to tell the story and find out whether it makes sense to them. [...] However, it's also important that they [the employees] are allowed to push back, uh, and say if you want digitization, could it not be ... (Interview with the Executive Board 2016)

At the same time, senior management describe the meetings as a huge success. What is interesting here is that senior management believe that they set the scene for an open communication environment. However, employees perceive it as a closed environment where you can't express your concerns without going unpunished since you "immediately get a pounding".

If employees don't want to take responsibility for giving critical feedback to management, it can also reinforce the trend towards a closed communication environment. This may be because employees need to appear in a positive light with management, which can be expressed in an exaggerated manifestation of agreement with management (Kjærbeck and Lundholt 2018a). Another reason may be that there is a higher likelihood that people express themselves if they get support from others (Bowen and Blackmon 2003). Social control also plays a role, as an employee wishes to maintain a social relationship with colleagues and therefore prefers to confirm rather than refute the group's opinions.

We find an example where all these mechanisms come into play in a medium-sized Danish organization, where for a long time the Executive Board had felt the employees need to appear in a positive light with management. It led to the following comments from the CFO to the CEO: "You say that sometimes there are some of the bosses who love to agree with me, and then we can sit and validate each other because they don't have that ability or the courage to say: I disagree!" Numerous researchers have offered suggestions as to why it may be attractive to agree both to management and colleagues, and we will examine those in the following section.

Different categories of organizational silence

Silent behaviour among employees can result in the following actions:

1. Exit.
2. Loyalty.
3. Neglect.
   (Monzani et al. 2016)

"Exit" refers to employees who choose to leave the organization and so avoid confronting the organization with their criticism. "Loyalty" refers to employees who patiently wait for the organization to address the problem without employee intervention. "Neglect" is about employees having passive behaviour, where they quietly withdraw from the organization by taking days off, getting to work late or dealing with personal matters during working hours.

The three concepts contrast with the category "voice", which refers to feedback where employees actively address issues within the organization, contributing to an open communication environment (Monzani et al. 2016: 247).

Researchers have identified four different kinds of silence:

1. Acquiescent.
2. Quiescent.
3. Prosocial silence.
4. Opportunistic silence.
   (Knoll and van Dick 2013)

Acquiescence occurs when the employee's opinion is not appreciated by management, i.e., the employees feel that management doesn't show interest in feedback. Consequently, the employee refrains from contributing with their input.

Quiescent occurs when the employee withholds relevant information to protect themselves. Maybe the employee has seen that feedback has had severe consequences for colleagues who have not held back. The employee remains silent for fear of ending up in the same situation.

When the employee withholds information to protect the organization or a colleague, it's a case of prosocial silence.

With opportunistic silence, the employee can see an advantage in withholding vital information for personal gain. It could, for example, be that the employee's own agenda was given lower priority if management considered it necessary to throw resources at other projects.

Voice

An employee can express their criticism in various ways. Researchers use the term "voice" to describe feedback, and they distinguish between two types:

1. Promotive.
2. Prohibitive.
    (Lin and Johnson 2015)

The promotive voice is about expressing ideas and suggestions to improve or optimize, while the prohibitive voice is about employees expressing concerns with the objective of preventing the organization from failing. Lind and Johnson's research shows that employees expressing a promotive voice, perform better and feel less run down than employees who practice prohibitive voice. This means that behaviour that is beneficial to the organization is not necessarily beneficial to the employee. Therefore, management has an important job to reward both types of feedback and create a culture where criticism is appreciated and a natural part of working life.

Organizational silence across cultures

Another source of organizational silence may be the employees' cultural backgrounds. There are some areas here that management must pay particular attention to if employees have a different cultural background, or if there is considerable geographical/cultural diversity among employees in an organization.

These may include language problems, which means that employees don't understand the message and therefore don't react as anticipated by management. Another problem can occur if there is a significant power gap between management and employees and if management also doesn't make it clear what expectations they have for the employees. As Mette Schnefeld, HR Business Partner at Danfoss, explains:

 But it's apparently also because the "contract" is unclear: What is expected of me as an employee, why do they come here to our location when they normally communicate in writing, what do they want to take away from here and so on. If it's not clearly articulated, the employees don't know what management's purposes and intentions are with this type of meeting, and they can't adjust to the anticipated behaviour. So, the "contract" must be clarified.

Many studies have confirmed that employees from countries with a big power gap (e.g., India, France and the Arab countries) tend to take the power gap between employees and managers for granted (Hofstede 1991; Morrison and Milliken 2000). This means that employees from these cultures are less likely to express their opinions to colleagues and management to avoid conflicts and direct confrontations (Morrison and Milliken 2000). In countries with a small power gap (e.g., Denmark, England and the Netherlands), as a starting point, one is more willing to make one's views known to the management. In these countries, employees also expect to have some degree of involvement.

It's essential to be aware that the mechanisms you put into play in the organization to break down organizational silence, don't, therefore, have the same effect in different cultures. Research shows that employees from countries with a big power gap, who can participate in decision-making, don't achieve greater job satisfaction or become more productive (Eylon and Au 1999). Instead, these types of employees perform better when they don't have to take part in the decision-making process. This result contrasts with countries with a small power gap, where we see increasing job satisfaction and productivity with increased involvement.

The key to breaking down organizational silence in countries with a big power gap is that management, in connection with involvement activities, directly encourages employees to give feedback (Huang et al. 2005).

In any communication situation, it's important to be open to that your expectations for behaviour and preferences will not always be met. In some organizations, there is, for instance, a strong culture that transcends national borders and organizational hierarchies, and where behaviour breaks with traditional patterns of behaviour. Common to all cultures is that management's conduct plays a crucial role if we are to create an open communication environment.

Why does management avoid feedback?

Ironically, managers often have a feeling that they continuously encourage employees to give feedback, but employees don't take up the call.

This can be explained by the concept of "double-blind leadership" (Hennestad 1990), which is managers consciously or unconsciously signalling that they actually don't have a sincere interest in listening to employees' opinions. So, although managers encourage employees to give feedback, their behaviour doesn't support the call, which makes it sound hollow to employees.

One explanation of double-blind leadership can be found in the fact that we humans are basically sensitive and critical of negative input that conflicts with our own self-image. In contrast, we intuitively assess positive feedback as valid (Tourish and Hargie 2004). This means that managers, for example, reject criticism based on employees' lack of understanding of administrative procedures and strategic initiatives.

It doesn't seem that managers are aware of how limited critical feedback actually is when the culture is characterized by a closed communication environment. In other words, they believe that any criticism there might be in the organization will reach them. Meanwhile, managers don't understand how their own behaviour can be a barrier to creating an open communication environment (Tourish and Robson 2006).

Research shows that influence is one of the most crucial parameters in relation to creating communication upwards (Tourish and Robson 2006; Kipnis and Schmidt 1988). In addition, both senior management and the direct manager's transparency is crucial in terms of how open the rest of the organization's members dare to be. Many researchers have concluded that even though senior management plays a significant role, it's the immediate manager's attitude to organizational silence that is most crucial in relation to employees' courage to openly express critics (Vakola and Bouradas 2005; Morrison and Milliken 2000). This may be partly explained by the possible identification between the manager and employee. Such identification can occur through, among other things, *authentic leadership*

Authentic leadership and transparency

Authenticity in leadership is generally about the relationship between the manager's behaviour, one's own values and the values of the organization (Monzani et al. 2016). The authentic manager is true to themselves and their own beliefs and has a high degree of credibility, making the manager a compelling role model for employees who in the same way seek to internalize and integrate their authentic manager's values and behaviour in their own self-understanding. The higher the degree of personal identification between the manager and employee, the more open the communication environment will prove to be.

Research also shows that employees are more likely to be whistle-blowers – employees' exposure of illegal or immoral actions within the organization – in organizations where they have a high degree of identification with their managers (Liu et al. 2015).

Authentic leadership has not only a critical impact on the communication environment but also on employees' perception of the organization's reputation. Research demonstrates how authentic leadership and the resulting communication behaviours affect employees' perception of the organization's reputation positively (Men 2014). We can also mention increased confidence, engagement, contentment, job satisfaction and performance as results of authentic leadership (ibid.). The explanation can be partly found in the realization that authenticity is often triggered by open communication as the authentic manager constantly invites dialogue and seeks feedback (Walumbwa et al. 2010). Men (2014) has demonstrated a correlation between authenticity and transparency, as authentic managers are characterized by them openly sharing information with employees while signifying their own opinions to the messages. This kind of transparency triggers an open communication between employees, who also dare to stand by their opinion and contribute with ideas to management.

The research also shows a correlation between organizational transparency and employees' trust in the organization. Organizations that share extensive information with their employees – good and bad – and encourage involvement and ownership of the messages have an increased likelihood of being seen in a positive light by employees (Rawlins 2008).

Measurement of the communication environment

The open communication environment, as mentioned previously, is a prerequisite for dialogue and meaningful creative communication. It's hard to imagine that as a manager, you can be successful in a dialogue-based approach if each manager has not established an open communication environment in the department. But how do you assess whether the communication environment is sufficiently open in a particular organization?

In an extensive study, Vakola and Bourades (2005) identified three dimensions of what they call the organizations' silence climate with a view to uncovering the dimensions' impact on employee silence, organizational engagement and job satisfaction. The study was based on a wide range of opinions and questions that employees must assess the truth of. The following questions and statements were included, among others:

- If you express disagreement in relation to organization-related problems, do you then risk that it leads to negative consequences from senior management?
- If you express disagreement in relation to organization-related problems, will you then be considered as trouble-maker by senior management?
- If you disagree with organization-related problems, is it then perceived by senior management as a lack of loyalty?
- In this organization, employees can freely express themselves.
- Senior management encourages employees to express their disagreement with organization-related problems.
- How often do you express disagreement regarding department-related problems to your boss?
- How often do you express disagreement regarding organizational-related problems to your boss?
- How often do you express disagreement regarding your job to your boss?
- How problem-free can you express disagreement in relation to department-related problems to your boss?

- How problem-free can you express disagreement regarding your job to your boss?
- How often do you express your disagreement regarding problems related to job satisfaction such as pay, working conditions, etc., to your boss?

The questions and statements are examples of how to examine the communication environment in an organization. It's a firm basis for ongoing leadership communication to gain insight into the communication environment in the organization. In this way, you obtain an insight into the degree of openness and where there is a need to make an extra effort. Here it may be appropriate to have some thoughts on how the communication environment can be more open if this is a wish. If you as a manager want to work to achieve a more dialogue-based communication environment, you can use different tactics.

The road to an open communication environment

When a manager has created an overview of the characteristics of the communication environment in the organization, the communication environment can be moved in a more open direction based on the following tactics:

1. *Change employees' mindset*: Most of us decide whether we should express our opinions based on a risk assessment. Studies show that employees who are good at expressing their opinions, first consider the associated risks by *not* speaking. If you can influence the employees' mindset in this direction, it increases the chances that employees give feedback.
2. *Work with your own feelings and opinions*: The reason that employees often experience feedback as negative, is usually that the manager is irritated, angry or indignant. Employees react to these feelings. Therefore, it's vital that you as a manager retain an open mind and consider employees as rational and decent people.

3. *Getting employees to feel secure*: Employees become defensive if they feel insecure. A prerequisite for the open communication environment is that as a manager, you explain your own positive motives and so the employees feel respected. When employees feel respected, and they trust the manager's motives, they lower their guard and start to listen, even if the topic is unpleasant.
4. *Invite dialogue*: When a manager has created a secure environment, you can communicate your messages and invite dialogue. Here it's crucial to encourage employees not to agree unconditionally (adapted from Maxfield 2016).

The ten inspiration points of involvement leadership communication (see Chapter 7, page 79) can be used to get employees to contribute to an open communication environment.

As this chapter has shown, there are many mechanisms that affect the communication environment. Overall, there are two conditions that must be in place. Firstly, it's technically possible for employees to express their opinions through various communication channels. Many new ways have emerged to give your opinion with the development of social media.

Secondly, it's vital that senior management and the direct manager support an open communication environment. If not, you can have many channels without it resulting in employees communicating freely. In the next section, we will look at the potential of social media in terms of creating a more open communication environment.

Communication environment and social media

In step with the changing media landscape in which social media enables all employees across levels and the organization to engage in dialogue, there is also an increased need among employees for a more open communication environment. This led Guldbrandsen and Just (2011) to talk about the "collaborative paradigm" where everyone can contribute and create meaning.

Today we see how social media is increasingly becoming a central communication platform, not only in the private sphere but also at work. This development means that more and more organizations are using social media within the organization as a hub for dialogue and sharing data. Blogs, microblogging, wikis, social networking, podcasting, video and photos, instant messaging and discussion forums are some of the most important forms of communication (Friedl and Verčič 2011: 85).

Social media platforms can help to reduce the power gap while giving managers a platform from which they can build and maintain relationships with a large group of employees across departments and national borders (Huy and Shipilov 2012). The media platform can create relationships because social media allows you to give immediate feedback, to engage in interaction and target communication to a specific audience. It's precisely such social characteristics that help to create a more symmetrical communication.

The development of social media has also meant that the organization's communication can no longer be/is controlled centrally. Upper management, the communication department or selected spokespeople in the organization no longer have a patent on communication. In contrast, all stakeholders can communicate alternative and critical views on the company's operations and decisions.

In technical terms, the terms "univocality" and "multivocality" are used to describe how communication works (Balmer 2001).

Univocality refers to the centrally controlled communication that aims to unify communication to avoid ambiguity in relation to the organization's messages.

Multivocality instead embraces the polyphony that social media, among other things, allows. Multivocality is an expression of that communication on social media is established through a collective creation (Guldbrandsen and Just 2011), which means that communication depends on whether management can create an open communication environment, where employees are willing to take part in online communication.

A prerequisite for achieving an open communication environment where employees make their opinions known, is also that employees have confidence in not only the technology, but just as much in management's intentions with the communication: Management must support them and acknowledge the employees for expressing their opinions, even critical ones (Huang et al. 2013: 121).

Despite social media's massive potential in terms of creating engagement and contributing to an open communication environment, according to a survey, only 12% of employees feel that their organizations use social media in a way that employees can express their opinions and concerns (Gifford 2013: 14). This trend is supported by a report written by Gatehouse (2017). The report shows that just over half of employees who use social media find it effective. If there is, for example, too many platforms in use, some employees feel that it's difficult to navigate around them. As Mette Schnefeld, HR Business Partner at Danfoss, says:

> Our preliminary experience with the various platforms that we have at Danfoss is that it creates complexity for some employees that over time we now have many platforms: sales force chatting groups, SharePoint sites for different teams, Facebook groups, intranets, Cornerstone, WhatsApp groups and so on. This actually increases people's confusion with where to seek information as searching for information for some employees is still the primary reason why they use the media that is available.

The Director of Gatehouse, Lee Smith, also points out that social media, such as Yammer, isn't exploited enough as they are often launched by the IT department and so end up as a "platform looking for a cause" (Wright 2017). Therefore, it's vital that employees are adequately informed about the purpose of the internal potential of social media. It's also important that management is involved and show the way. If management doesn't use the social networks themselves and so show what they can be used for, there is a high probability that many of the employees also won't use them.

Finally, there may be significant differences in how social media is used in different parts of the world (for example, see Kim et al. 2011).

Part II: From theory to practice

By Anette Uldall

To gain insight into the theories is the first step towards being able to practice leadership communication, but the insight alone does not make the job any easier. There is a need for a straightforward and effective tool to move from theory to practice.

The Leadership Communication Tool Kit (Lundholt and Uldall 2010) is our take on how individual managers can strengthen their leadership communication in practice. It's an effective tool that the manager can use, partly to prepare a specific communication task and partly to devise an internal communication strategy (see Chapter 9).

We developed the Leadership Communication Tool Kit and the corresponding training concept when we worked as communication advisors at Danfoss, and since 2011, we have trained hundreds of managers in both private and public companies in the use of the tool kit. For inspiration for the readers who are working to improve manager communication skills, Chapter 10 describes the training concept.

To illustrate leadership communication in practice, through a case from Danfoss, Chapter 11 will show how the company communicated a new strategy to more than 23,000 employees, and improved the leadership communication skills of managers by, among other things, using the Leadership Communication Tool Kit. Although the examples of leadership communication are based on a large global company, we are confident that the elements of this case may also be useful in other, smaller organizations.

We will refer to the theory part in the chapters, so that theoretical concepts are elaborated and compared with practice.

Chapter 9

The Leadership Communication Tool Kit

Thorough preparation is the key to any successful communication. The Leadership Communication Tool Kit consists of the main elements that a manager must consider in planning communication professionally to have greater success with communication. This applies both to the specific communication task, and when the manager must devise an internal communication strategy.

In this chapter, we will review the elements of the tool kit and give an example of how the tool kit has been used to plan a specific communication. We will also show how management has used the tool kit to devise an internal communication strategy.

Communication's seven elements

In its pure form, professional communication is all about adapting communication to the target group. This requires 1) a thorough knowledge of the target groups that are in play in each situation, and 2) an awareness of what you want to achieve with your communication. As the sender, you must also 3) prepare a clear message, 4) consider the target groups' reactions, 5) select the communication channels and 6) the time and 7) have an explicit agreement on who is responsible for communication. These aspects are the seven elements of communication, and together they make up the Leadership Communication Tool Kit. When you open the tool kit, you will be guided through all seven elements, ensuring that you have considered all aspects before the actual communication.

The template and a leaflet describing the Leadership Communication Tool Kit can be downloaded from the book's site: *samfundslitteratur.dk/leadershipcommunication*, or via the QR code below.

Figure 15. The Leadership Communication Tool Kit. Source: Lundholt and Uldall 2010.

1. Target group

The first communication element is the target group. Who are you going to communicate to?

It's important to start by reflecting on whom the communication is aimed at, as it may ultimately affect the message. It's our experience that managers' focus on the message often tends to overshadow the work with the target group, which may result in the communication not meeting the group's needs.

Understand your target group

The questions in Figure 16 on the following page should help the sender to understand the target group's needs.

By completing Figure 16, you can reflect on who you are communicating with, the target group's relationship to the sender, as well as the target group's preferences. These factors may vary from employee to employee. Some employees have a good relationship with their manager, whereas others may have a more strained relationship, etc. Other factors such as preferences for numbers, graphs and other illustrations can also be relevant to relate to. There may also be messages that have different consequences for individual target groups and this, in turn, will affect the formulation of the message and the communication channel.

Many speak today about communication noise – too much irrelevant, time-consuming communication. Therefore, it's essential to relate to whether the message is even relevant for all target groups (see the section on relevant communication in Chapter 3, page 48).

It's also important not to define target groups that are too broad. One example is: If a target group is the entire sales team of 100 salespeople all over the world, the manager should consider whether this group should be divided into several target groups; according to markets, regions, countries and so on. It's not certain that the message must be the same and sent out via the same channel to all 100 salespeople, as there may be differences in communicating to salespeople in Denmark, France or China. Perhaps the message is more relevant and has greater consequences for salespeople in China than in Denmark, and so the message needs to be tailored for each of these target groups, just as the communication channel must be carefully considered, which we will go into later.

Understand your target group	Target group #1	Target group #2	Target group #...
What does your target group already know?			
What relevance does your message have for the target group?			
What would they like to know?			
What do they think they know?			
What is new to them?			
What can prevent them from doing what you ask them?			
What relationship do you have with your target group?			
Is there a case of an equal relationship between you and your target group?			
Does your target group regard you as trustworthy?			
What is the target group's opinion of you?			
Is your target group comfortable or uncomfortable with respect to unknown parameters?			
Does your target group prefer an indirect or direct style of communication?			

Figure 16. Understand your target group. Source: Lundholt and Uldall 2010.

Direct, indirect and not affected target groups

It's also important to relate to who will be *directly affected*, *indirectly affected* or *not affected* by the changes that are to be communicated. Some employees may be directly affected by a decision that, for example, will result in changes to processes or procedures, new premises, a change of work duties or other consequences that affect their working lives. This group of employees can be categorized as "directly affected".

For other employees, the message doesn't have specific consequences, and they will be able to continue their regular work without major changes. We can categorize this group of employees as "indirectly affected". Although the indirectly affected don't experience specific changes in their daily work, they may find that in the future they work with other colleagues from the department affected. They may be baffled by the decision if they don't get information almost simultaneously with those affected. Therefore, it's crucial that the indirectly affected are also considered a key target group.

The "not affected" target group must also be considered. It's a group that isn't affected at all, but who require information to ensure that everyone has received the same fundamental message. This prevents rumours and misinterpretations in the organization, which in turn can lead to unrest and uncertainty. Examples may be larger rounds of redundancies, organizational changes, and the like.

2. Objective

When the target groups are defined, the objective of the communication is determined. What do you want to *achieve* with the communication? Why communicate? Is it pure information? Must employees change their behaviour? Or is it a question of getting the employees' support for and ownership of a new strategy? The list can be quite extensive.

In the same communication task, the objective of communicating may vary according to the target group. Some target groups only need to be informed, other target groups must be convinced of the message, and others must take ownership of a major change in their daily work.

The manager should be aware of the communication *objective* and *form* of communication if communication is to succeed. It may be useful here to return to the graph in Chapter 4:

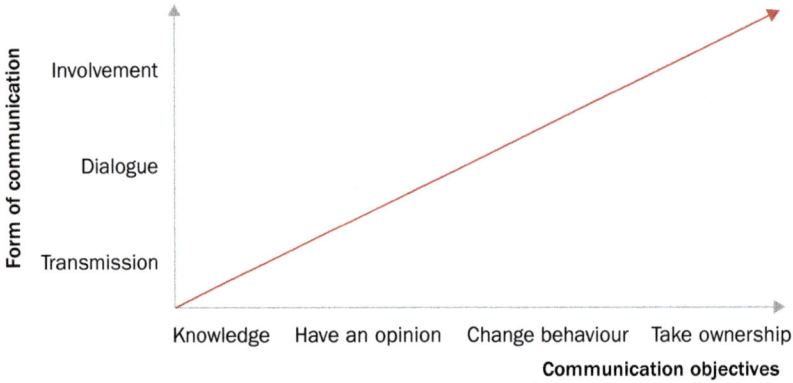

Figure 17. Form of communication and communication objectives.

This graph shows the relationship between the communication objective and form: When the objective of communication is that employees merely need to have knowledge of the message, it's enough to transmit the message through one-way communication. This can be practical information such as a new colleague starts on Monday, that the date of the team meeting has changed or that staff appraisals will take place in early June this year.

However, as soon as the objective of the communication is to change opinions, change behaviour or even take ownership, the form of communication moves over to dialogue and involvement.

Should employees, for example, understand the new strategy for the company, it requires that managers engage in dialogue with their team and ensure that employees feel comfortable about asking clarifying questions. This gives managers the opportunity to deepen and relate the strategy to employees' daily work and the changes that a new strategy might cause.

When employees take ownership, as is often the case with major changes, managers, together with the employees, must interpret these changes and formulate a common message – what we call involvement. Examples of changes can range from fundamental changes of work processes to major organizational changes and the introduction of new duties. In such cases, managers and employees must formulate the message together that answers the question: "What does this mean for our daily work?"

The three forms of communication each meet their respective objectives: In the form of communication *transmission*, the target groups must receive the message, in the form of communication *dialogue*, they must understand the message, and in the form of communication *involvement*, they must interpret the message and so take ownership. To check whether the objective of the communication is met, the manager can ask the target groups some questions. Let us look again at the questions related to the three forms of communication:

	Form of communication	Question
1	*Transmission* of information from the manager to employees	Did you receive my message?
2	*Dialogue* between the manager and employees	Did you understand my message?
3	*Involvement* of employees	How do you understand/interpret my message?

Figure 18. Form of communication and questions.

Especially the last question: "How do you understand/interpret my message" requires that the manager lets employees reflect on the message by asking open questions.

For example, when a department must work with new tasks, the manager could open the meeting with a brief review of the new tasks and then invite dialogue. To get employees to reflect and thereby contribute to a common understanding, the manager could then ask the following questions:

- What is your immediate reaction when I mention the new tasks?
- What do you think about the new tasks?
- What does this mean for our current tasks?
- What is required of us to perform these tasks?
- What obstacles might we encounter?
- What can we get out of performing the tasks?
- How do you see the relationship between the new tasks and our common strategy?

The manager's job is primarily to take a step back and listen to employees' reflections. Next, together with the employees, the manager can formulate the message that expresses the common understanding of the new tasks, and so ensure that employees support and take ownership of these changes.

Some managers will believe they don't have time for this form of communication. Nevertheless, it's a good investment if you want employees to take ownership.

You can read more about forms and objectives of communication in Chapters 4, 5, 6 and 7.

3. Message

Many managers immediately throw themselves into formulating a message when they must plan a communication. The message is the third element in the tool kit. And with good reason. When you don't know the target group and the objective of communicating, it's harder to be precise in your message.

Formulation of the message also depends on the form of communication. When it comes to transmission and dialogue, the message is formulated before it's communicated, whereas the message in the form of communication involvement, is formulated together with the target groups.

The table on the following page shows when the message is formulated prior to the communication or in collaboration with the target group – depending on the form of communication.

	Form of communication	Question	Message
1	*Transmission* of information from the manager to employees	Did you receive my message?	The message is formulated in advance of the communication
2	*Dialogue* between the manager and employees	Did you understand my message?	
3	*Involvement* of employees	How did you understand/interpret my message?	The message is created in the communication situation in collaboration between the manager and the target group

Figure 19. Form of communication, question and message.

When it comes to the forms of communication transmission and dialogue, the key message is formulated prior to communication. Here it's important to be concise and cut right to the bone. As a rule, we should formulate the three main points that the target group should remember and that all further communication should be based on.

However, it's often a painful process to cut right to the bone. Here it helps to answer these questions: What, why, who, how and when? As well as limiting the key message to a few points. See the example on page 120.

When the key message is in place, it can be tailored to the target groups:

- Start with the key message, so the target groups immediately get an idea of what it's about.
- Then elaborate the key message with facts, examples and details that are important to each target group.
- Explain how the message correlates to a strategy (the common thread).
- Explain in more detail what it means for the individual target group.

- And finally: Repeat the key message so that the target group remembers it.

It's often necessary to formulate different messages depending on the needs of the individual target groups. However, the key message is the same for all target groups.

It's also at this stage that the manager must consider the use of the appeal forms ethos (credibility/trust), logos (logical reasoning) and pathos (talk to the target group's emotions) and then work with the language, so that the message is consistent, captures the target group's attention and convinces them.

Pathos is an appeal form that many managers shy away from slightly. However, it can be very powerful when used wisely. This quote which is ascribed to, among others, American author Maya Angelou describes the effect of pathos: "I've learned that people will forget what you said, people will forget what you did, but people will never forget how you made them feel."

When the form of communication is *involvement*, the message must not be formulated in advance. It happens in the communication situation together with the employees. As previously mentioned, it's necessary that you as a manager take a step back and invite reflection and dialogue to interpret and formulate the message jointly. This requires that you put the logos appeal form in the background and make room for a more ethos and pathos orientated communication.

The manager can achieve this by following these ten points of inspiration:

1. Be value-neutral.
2. Accept feedback and criticism.
3. Listen rather than convince.
4. Accept different worldviews.
5. Be curious.
6. Be investigative.
7. Be concerned with understanding what the other person understands.

8. Show sincere interest in the other person and their concerns.
9. Focus on employees' relationship to change.
10. Listen for the unsaid.

You can read more about this process in the "When the message is formulated in the communication situation" section in Chapter 7.

4. Anticipated reactions

As mentioned in the theoretical part, the target groups interpret the message in every communication situation based on personal experience.

Many managers have been in a situation where they have been surprised by the target group's reactions, primarily because they haven't thought through the possible reactions in advance. If you don't do this, you, as a manager have put yourself in a situation where you appear uncertain, and it may result in you appearing untrustworthy and therefore you won't experience that the message resonates with employees.

However, it can be problematic to predict how a message will be received. Here it's advantageous to test your communication, for example, on managerial colleagues who know the target group and ask for feedback. In this way, you can adjust your communication in relation to the target group. Meaningful questions to ask the selected recipients could be:

- Is the communication relevant?
- Is the message understandable?
- How do you understand the message?
- What is your immediate reaction to the message?
- Is there anything that should be deleted or added?

This little test can provide crucial input concerning the target group. If the manager has also prepared for different reactions – from enthusiasm to opposition, even anger – then already in his message he can pre-empt the reactions through his choice of words and by proactively answering the questions that these reactions might result in. The manager can also prepare some possible questions and answers, which they can use in a communication situation. See an example of questions and answers on page 121.

5. Channel

The first four elements are now in place:

- Target group(s).
- Objective and the form of communication.
- Whether the message must be formulated prior to or in the communication situation. And in cases where the message must be formulated in advance, the key message is formulated and tailored to the individual target groups.

The fifth element is the communication channel. It's the media that you have available, ranging from e-mail, intranet, bulletin boards, social media to soapbox meetings, department meetings and personal meetings – including online meetings.

The list of communication channels is extensive, and in conjunction with a focus on effective communication, it's not surprising that e-mail is a preferred communication media. It's relatively simple, and you can reach a large target group in a short time while ensuring that all recipients receive the same message at the same time.

From a communication perspective, however, there are other factors that are crucial to whether the communication is effective or not. In its simple form, successful communication is about the sender achieving the desired objectives. Therefore, it's vital that the *form* of communication and communication *channel* are linked.

There is a difference whether the sender chooses spoken or written communication. When selecting a communication channel that allows you to communicate face-to-face, then you will have a higher possibility together with your target group of achieving a common understanding of the message, even if the communication channel, for example, is an online meeting. Written communication doesn't have the same possibilities.

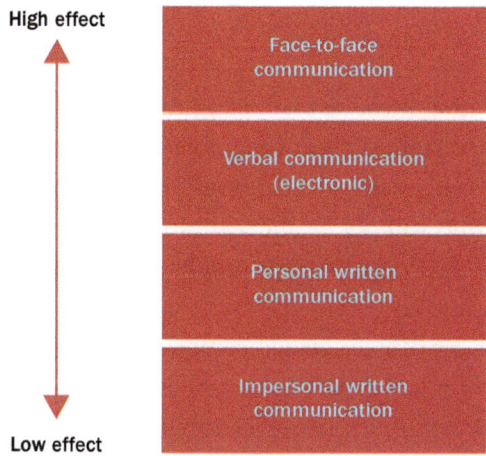

Figure 20. Spoken versus written communication.

The figure illustrates that the effect of the communication varies, depending on whether the message is communicated verbally or in writing.

If it's pure information from the manager to employees that doesn't require dialogue, an e-mail or a post on the intranet is an excellent channel to use.

If the purpose is instead to get employees to understand and accept the message, you will need to use other channels such as face-to-face communication (meetings). This may be in connection with major organizational changes and redundancies, or to ensure employees support a new plan or strategy. If you wish to engage in dialogue with employees, social media can in some cases be a viable channel, for example, following a face-to-face meeting where you have communicated the message and then invite dialogue. However, this assumes that you actively participate in the dialogue.

When the purpose is to get employees to take ownership of new work processes or a new strategy, and the form of communication is therefore *involvement*, then the most effective communication channel will be face-to-face meetings. It can also be online meetings, which, however, requires a good relationship and an open communication environment. You can read more about the communication environment in Chapter 8.

6. Timing

The communication must be planned so that the target groups receive the message at the right time. For example, in the case of major organizational changes where the affected employees must be informed before the colleagues who will not be affected by the change. You should also be considered whether the message collides with other messages, as this may create confusion.

An example: a privately-owned company must implement a major reorganization of many departments where a number of staff are made redundant. It's a change that involves employees worldwide. Some employees will be affected by the organizational change by having new duties. Others are affected because they are made redundant. In order to avoid unnecessary turmoil and misunderstanding, the message is communicated to the indirectly affected and not affected employees immediately after the affected employees have received the message. Therefore, the timing is vital in relation to that communication must take place simultaneously to everyone throughout the world, and before the press is informed, and it requires meticulous planning. The employees have also just received the message that a number of employees have been hired in other departments. Therefore, it's essential that the background for the decision to employ more people in other departments is also explained in the message that employees receive regarding this reorganization and staff reduction, so there is no confusion and frustration.

7. Responsibility

Responsibility for communication lies with the manager. Communication can't be outsourced, as it's part of management responsibility. Of course, this doesn't mean that you can't get support from communication advisors and HR partners.

It's senior management's responsibility to communicate the company's overall strategic direction and to ensure that employees' immediate manager conveys the message.

It's the immediate manager's responsibility to communicate the strategic decisions while explaining the importance of these decisions for the department, team and individual employees.

The Communication Diamond – interaction between the elements

The seven elements appear as a linear process illustrated in Figure 15 (page 104) and described in the section immediately following. The key to professional communication is, however, to understand the interaction and synergy between the seven elements, illustrated in this model:

Figure 21. The Communication Diamond. Source: Lundholt and Uldall 2010.

The model illustrates how to compare the elements from all directions. In preparing a communication task, you follow the process step-by-step, i.e. you begin by defining the target group (element 1) and continue to work with the other elements step-by-step. However, you will often find that you have to go back and re-examine, for example, the target groups and form of communication (objective and channel – elements 2 and 5), because in considering the anticipated reactions (element 4) or the message (element 3) you discover that you have overlooked a target group or acknowledged that you must use another form of communication. Therefore, make sure that you have considered all aspects. The following types of questions may be helpful to compare the elements from all directions:

- What does it mean for my choice of the form of communication channel and formulating the message that there is pure information to multiple target groups?
- What does it mean for my message, timing and choice of the form of communication and channel that I need to both communicate to those, directly and indirectly, affected, and that the message will most likely create frustration among those directly affected?
- What does it mean for my choice of the form of communication, channel and timing that my objective of the communication is that one of the target groups take ownership of the change we are facing?

Example of a specific communication task

The following paragraphs show an example of a specific communication task. The communication plan is drawn up based on the Leadership Communication Tool Kit prior to communication about an organizational change at Danfoss Drives. The names in this example have been made anonymous. Let us begin with an overview of the aspects that management had considered in the preparation phase.

As stated in the communication plan, management has defined nine target groups: Management groups (both direct, indirect and not affected), employee representatives (not affected), coordination committee (directly affected) and employee groups (directly affected and not affected).

THE LEADERSHIP COMMUNICATION TOOL KIT | 119

Target groups	Objective	Message	Anticipated Reactions	Channel	Timing	Responsible
Who will receive the message?	What do I want to achieve by sending the message?	What is the key message?	How can the target group be expected to react to the message?	Which channel to choose?	When should the message be conveyed?	Who is responsible for developing and communicating the message?
DDLT & SCLT & Local site management	Information and preparation	**Organizational change within Danfoss Drives Global Supply Chain** • Since our merger, we have had two Global Operations and Logistics functions. Now we are ready to announce the next step. • As of October 1st, 2016 TL, Vice President will head the Global Logistics function within Global Supply Chain. • As of October 1, 2016 TH, Vice President will head the Global Operations function within Danfoss Drives. During September, Txxx and Txxx will continue the process of getting their global teams in place and we will announce the next level in the beginning of October 2016. Until then the reporting structure will remain the same.	Positive	Email incl. Drives news, Q&A's and com. plan	Monday August 29 at 12.00 CET	N
Factory managers & GOL team	Information and preparaton		What about my job?	Meeting & email incl. Drives news, Q&A's and com. plan	Monday August 29 at 15.00 CET	T & T
Employee representatives DK +FI	Information and buy-in		Positive	Email incl. Drives news, Q&A's and com. plan	Tuesday August 30 morning CET	M & K
Workers council DK + FI	Information and buy-in		Overall positive, however worried that there will be job cuts – see Q&A	Face-to-face or email incl. Drives news, Q&A's and com. plan	Tuesday August 30 morning CET	T & K
DK Local site management	Information and preparation		Positive	Email incl. Drives news, Q&A's and com. plan	Tuesday August 30 morning CET	T
Affected employees in Logistic dep. & Operations dep.	Information and buy-in		Worried that there will be job custs – see Q&A	Face-to-face department meeting with Txxx & Txxx	Tuesday August 30	T & T
Affected employees in Logistic dep. & Operations dep	Buy-in/commitment		Worried that there will be job cuts – see Q&A	Face-to-face	Tuesday August 30 all day 1:1's with TL	T
Global S/C news	Information		Overall neutral	Global S/C news	Wednesday August 31 at 9.00 CET	N
Drives news	Information		Overall neutral	Drives news	Wednesday August 31 at 9.30 CET	N

Figure 22. Communication plan. Source: Danfoss.

The objective of communicating with some of the target groups (indirect and not affected) is information, so, therefore, the communication form transmission is chosen, and the communication channels are e-mail and intranet. In contrast, the objective of communicating to other target groups (directly affected) is to gain the acceptance of these target groups (buy-in) of this organizational change, and here you choose dialogue as the form of communication, while the communication channel is face-to-face.

In relation to timing, the managers of the organization are involved the day before the communication takes place to the directly affected employees. All managers received a communication package consisting of the communication plan (see Figure 22), the core message and the question/answer document (see Figures 23 and 24). The indirectly affected managers received information via e-mail from senior management in production, whereas the directly affected managers were involved via dialogue with senior management. It gave them time to prepare for the subsequent dialogue with employees.

The following morning senior management informed employee representatives and the coordination committee, as they must be informed of upcoming changes. Then the two senior managers, who in future will lead the organizations, communicated the change to the directly affected employees at the dialogue meetings. As middle managers had been involved the day before, they were now ready to also have a dialogue with the employees after meeting with senior managers.

Based on the key message, the following message was sent to all employees in the organization the day after via intranet for information, i.e. transmission (see below). Targeted messages were also prepared for the other target groups as set out in the communication plan.

Message:
Organizational change within Danfoss Drives Global Supply Chain

Since our merger, we have had two Global Operations and Logistics functions – one for the former PE sites and one for the former Vacon sites – to stay focused on our daily business and customer service. Now we are ready to announce the next step within Operations & Logistics in Global Supply Chain.

As of October 1st, 2016 TL, Vice President will head the Global Logistics function within Global Supply Chain. The Logistics organization focuses on that the processes and practices are designed so that customer requirements are met in the most cost-optimized manner. It is a process development organization with an order-to-cash approach and it will continuously utilize the capabilities provided by One ERP. H and V will continue to report to T.

As of October 1, 2016 TH, Vice President will head the Global Operations function within Danfoss Drives. T will be responsible for operations in all factories in Danfoss Drives. All factory managers in Danfoss Drives will report to T as of October 1st, 2016.

T. H. will not continue in his role as DK site Manager but M. T., Vice President, Design Center DK and DE will take over this role in future as of October 1st.

Both T and T will continue to be part of the Supply Chain Management Team (SCLT).

"In Global Supply Chain we constantly strive to increase our competitiveness by being best-in-class in terms of quality and delivery performance thus improving customer satisfaction and at the same time remaining cost-competitive. With the new future setup we strengthen the focus on our Global Logistics and Global Operations and we have dedicated resources in both positions to support our strategy", says M. S., Senior Vice President Global Supply Chain.

During September, T. and T. will continue the process of getting their global teams in place and we will announce the next level in the beginning of October 2016. Until then the reporting structure will remain the same.

Figure 23. Shared information via the intranet. Source: Danfoss.

The key message here is marked in red in the text to illustrate how it was used. Based on anticipated reactions, a question/answer document was also prepared that managers could use in a communication situation.

Q&As – forwarded to all managers for preparation

1. Why do you dedicate one ressource for the Global Logistics function?	We want to strengthen the focus on Global Operations
2. You state that T and T will now start the process of getting their global teams in place – when are you ready to announce the next level?	We will announce the next level in the beginning of October as soon as we are ready
3. Will our TS implementation be affected by these changes?	No. The ownership will follow the new structure
4. How will this affect the budget process for 2017?	T will head the budget discussions on factory sites and T for the Logistics function
5. Will all employees affected be offered new jobs?	We do not foresee any cuts in jobs in relation to this organizational change, and we will do our utmost to relocated and offer all affected colleagues other jobs
6. Will there be a job guarantee?	No
7. Do you have a strategy in place for the Global Logistics function?	We are working on a strategy and we will communicate this together with our S/C perspective end November
8. Will T continue as DK Site Manager	No, M T from R&D will take over as DK Site Manager
9. Where will T be based	T will be based in Finland
10. Will this change affect our current global footprint	This organizational change has no impact on our global footprint

Figure 24. Questions and answers. Source: Danfoss.

These questions and answers were sent to the managers before the communication took place.

The example shows how to get a grip on a specific communication task using the Leadership Communication Tool Kit and to be thoroughly prepared for it.

The tool kit can also be used to develop a communication strategy for internal leadership communication, and we will review this in the next section.

A tool kit for an internal communication strategy

An internal communication strategy gives the manager an overview of who they communicate with (target groups), for what purpose (objective), through which channels and how often. With this strategy in hand, the manager – after having coordinated it with the target groups

– can better ensure that the communication is targeted and ongoing so that the target groups are informed and involved to the degree that is relevant to them.

When you as a manager work with an internal communication strategy for leadership communication, you must work with most of the elements in the Leadership Communication Tool Kit. We will look at them one by one.

1. Target group

The first element is the target groups. Who do you communicate with? And who will you communicate with in the future? Managers already communicate with employees and colleagues in the management team, but very few have a firm plan for when they communicate with them. There could also be other target groups that you as a manager want to talk to. It might be senior management, other management teams or project groups.

2. Objective

Next, the manager must consider why they want to communicate to these target groups. Is the objective to keep engagement high among employees? Does the manager want other management teams and project groups involved when it comes to the department's plans? Will the manager inform senior management of the department's goals and achievements? There may be many objectives.

3. Message

In this element, the manager must consider the type of message they want to convey to the target groups. It could be the status of objectives and achievements, major projects or an informal chat about how things are going.

4. Anticipated reactions

The fourth element – anticipated reactions – the manager can't obviously take these into account in a communication strategy, as they depend on the communication itself, i.e. the content of the messages you want to convey, and these are continually changing. Therefore, the manager must first consider the anticipated reactions from the target groups once they have prepared for the communication situation.

5. Channel

The communication channel is the fifth element in the development of the communication strategy.

Often, managers have face-to-face staff meetings in the calendar, but they mainly use them to inform. Is it effective when instead they could simply have sent an e-mail with the same information? Or do they, in fact, wish to be in dialogue with employees, but don't take the opportunity?

Therefore, it's essential to consider the target groups and objective of the communication, before the manager decides on the communication channel.

If they just want to *inform*, an e-mail or a post on the intranet would be enough (see Chapter 5).

If, on the other hand, the manager wants to enter into *dialogue* with employees, then a meeting – either face-to-face or online – is the most natural communication channel (see Chapter 6). If you have established an open communication environment, social media can also be an excellent communication channel. However, it's crucial that the manager actively participates in dialogue in order to get the desired effect (see Chapter 8 on the way to an open communication environment).

If the manager wants middle managers to communicate their message to employees, it's imperative that the manager spends time with their middle managers to involve them and create meaning in interaction. See Chapter 3 on cascade communication and Chapter 7 on involvement. In this way, the manager can equip middle managers for the job, and thus better ensure that messages are correctly communicated.

As mentioned earlier in this chapter, a communication channel that gives a manager the ability to communicate personally and verbally, gives them a greater opportunity, together with the target group, to achieve a common understanding of the message, even if the communication channel is an online meeting or a telephone conversation. Written communication doesn't have the same possibilities.

6. Timing

In this element, the manager can plan when they want to communicate. It could be every month or every week, or immediately after senior management has communicated the key messages each quarter. It depends on the need for communication with the target groups.

7. Responsibility

Under "responsibility", the manager must decide who has the primary responsibility to communicate to the target groups as defined in the communication strategy. Is it the manager them self? Or the entire management team?

Coordinate with the target groups

When the communication strategy is in place, it may be useful to review it together with the target groups to get their response to whether it makes sense to them, and then align the strategy with their expectations. This will ensure that leadership communication is targeted and relevant to the target groups.

Example of a communication strategy

The following example is an overview of the strategy of senior management's internal communication in 2015 to about 4,000 employees worldwide in the business area of Danfoss Power Electronics.

As stated in the strategy, the internal communication from senior management is aimed at four target groups: senior management, the extended management team, all managers and all employees. The objective of communicating in the senior management team, in the extended management team and to all managers was to find common ground about the decisions taken in accordance with the business strategy and equip managers to convey the strategic decisions to all employees.

Since the objective was to gain acceptance and involve employees, the communication channel was face-to-face meetings, which could also have been online meetings. The meetings took place every month in senior management and every quarter for the other management groups, and the director of the business area was responsible for this part of the communication assisted by a communication advisor.

Danfoss Power Electronics – communication strategy overview

	Target Group	Objective	Message	Anticipated reactions	Channel	Timing	Responsibility
	Who will receive the message?	What do I want to achieve by sending the message?	What is the key message?	How can the target group be expected to react?	Which channel to choose?	When should the message be conveyed?	Who is responsible for developing and communicating the message?
"Face-to-face"	Top management team	Business decisions and alignment	Current and stratetic business topics	-	Meetings	Monthly	Segment President/ Comm. advisor
	Extended top management team	Business decisions and updates, and alignment	Current and strategic business topics	-	Meetings	Quarterly	Segment President/ Comm. advisor
	All managers	Business updates based on BRM meetings	Business update and selected topics	-	Video, and Q&A virtual meeting	Quarterly	Segment President/ Comm. advisor
	All employees	Providing the big picture and business status	Business update and selected topics	-	Face-to-face meetings	Quarterly	All managers
Intranet	All employees	Information sharing	The good and "bad" stories Organizational updates	-	Intranet: • PENews • Did You Know • On the Frontpage	Ongoing (twice a week in four languages (DK, CN, US and DE)	All can contribute /Comm. Advisor

Figure 25. Communication strategy. Source: Danfoss 2015.

The meetings with employees also took place each quarter. Here it was the individual managers' responsibility to communicate the strategic decisions and involve staff.

Information was also continuously published on the intranet for all employees in several languages. The purpose was to share the good, as well as the not so good stories across the organization and everyone could contribute with their story.

Based on this strategy, the individual management teams in the business area could develop their own approaches for internal leadership communication using the tool kit. For example, in their communication strategy, they could take into account that every quarter, senior management communicated the status of the business and strategic plans to all managers and invited to dialogue management meetings. So, they could plan employee meetings immediately after these management meetings to communicate senior management's messages to employees and explain what it meant for the individual teams.

Chapter 10

Training gives leadership communication a boost

The Leadership Communication Tool Kit, which has been discussed in the two previous chapters, was launched at Danfoss in 2010. In connection with the launch, we developed material, together with HR Consultant Peter Braun, for training managers in the use of the Leadership Communication Tool Kit. More than 3,000 managers at both Danfoss and other companies have participated in these training sessions.

The purpose of the training is to improve managers' communication skills. The training is based on practical examples from managers' everyday life, so they can return to their department with a clear feeling that communication isn't rocket science, but it's about taking your starting point with the recipients of the message and target the communication accordingly.

Today, communication training is an integral part of the regular training offered to managers at Danfoss. It's run by Corporation Communications, which is responsible for adapting the concept and conducting the training. Managers are referred, for example, to the offer when managers in collaboration with HR partners develop a plan for each manager's skills development. According to Corporation Communications, demand is increasing and shows that there is still a need for improving manager's skills in the field of communication.

This chapter presents the communication training concept that we developed in 2011. We hope it can be an inspiration to you who are working to improve manager skills in Leadership Communication.

Step-by-step communication training

Most training sessions take about 4 hours and take place face-to-face in groups of about 25 managers from all levels of management. The content of the training follows this agenda:

Agenda

1. Why should communication be on the agenda?
2. My responsibility as a manager
3. The Leadership Communication Tool Kit
4. Create a communication plan
5. Devise a communication strategy

Figure 26. Agenda with the five steps in communication training. Source: Danfoss 2011.

1. Why should communication be on the agenda?

Managers get a brief introduction here to communication theory and especially some arguments for the need to focus on communication.

Communication advisors in charge of training, also show the latest results of the organization's employee satisfaction survey. It leads to a discussion about what the problems are in terms of communication.

Then the managers are challenged in their ability to communicate via a little exercise where some of the participants via a mobile phone in a separate room convey the construction of an abstract Lego model to their colleagues who must build a similar model. It usually only partially succeeds for the colleagues to build the model. Translated into everyday life, it shows managers how difficult communication can be when you choose the wrong communication channel and along the way you don't ensure that the message has been understood. The subsequent group discussion often shows that managers can recognize the pitfalls from their everyday lives.

2. My responsibility as a manager

Next, managers in the groups discuss their role and responsibilities in relation to communication and later present to the group. Many excellent ideas and debates arise from this exercise, and during the rest of the training, reference is made to this discussion. In this way, managers share their experiences and challenges.

One of these challenges is to communicate general messages from senior management to employees and put them into a relevant context. It's often here that the wheels come off because managers have not had the necessary dialogue themselves with *their* manager and don't immediately seek dialogue in a busy day. Therefore, they don't feel adequately prepared for the job.

Communication advisors put the spotlight on this challenge during the rest of the training and along the way point out that managers are also a target group for their senior manager. The manager's manager has a responsibility to equip them for the job, but at the same time, they also have a responsibility to obtain relevant communication from their management. The last point for many managers is a particular eye-opener and gives food for thought.

3. The Leadership Communication Tool Kit

The next part of the training is a brief review of the seven elements in the Leadership Communication Tool Kit (see Chapter 9 for a review of the model). Before the training, managers were asked to read the folder about the tool kit. During the training, they can ask clarifying questions.

4. Create a communication plan

With this tool in hand, managers must now devise a plan for a specific communication task. It can be a communication task that they have brought along or an example that the communication advisor has prepared.

When they have worked with the plan, the managers must present their message to the group, where the rest of the participants must "act as" the target group that each manager had defined. Then, each manager gets feedback from their colleagues and from the communication advisor, which in turn gives rise to excellent discussions and an exchange of experiences.

The manager already knows many of the elements of the tool kit, but it's obvious that they focus primarily on the message itself and not so much on the target groups and the targeted messages to these target groups. For many managers, it's also difficult to formulate a brief and precise key message. Therefore, the training mainly consists of developing their skills in these areas.

5. Devise a communication strategy

In the last part of the training, each manager devises their own communication strategy using the tool. The strategy should include a plan for communication in the department concerned, and it must be connected to the overall communication within the organization (see the example).

Many managers already have regular meetings with employees, but most have never prepared a proper strategy and presented it to employees to see whether the communication is sufficient. The managers take this task with them when they return after the training is completed. A communication strategy may look like Figure 27 (the example is an overall strategy for one of Danfoss' business areas).

At the end of the training, the managers are asked to say what three things they want to change, improve or introduce when they return to the department.

Danfoss Power Electronics – communication strategy overview

	Target Group	Objective	Message	Anticipated reactions	Channel	Timing	Responsibility
	Who will receive the message?	What do I want to achieve by sending the message?	What is the key message?	How can the target group be expected to react?	Which channel to choose?	When should the message be conveyed?	Who is responsible for developing and communicating the message?
"Face-to-face"	Top management team	Business decisions and alignment	Current and stratetic business topics	-	Meetings	Monthly	Segment President/ Comm. advisor
	Extended top management team	Business decisions and updates, and alignment	Current and strategic business topics	-	Meetings	Quarterly	Segment President/ Comm. advisor
	All managers	Business updates based on BRM meetings	Business update and selected topics	-	Video, and Q&A virtual meeting	Quarterly	Segment President/ Comm. advisor
	All employees	Providing the big picture and business status	Business update and selected topics	-	Face-to-face meetings	Quarterly	All managers
Intranet	All employees	Information sharing	The good and "bad" stories Organizational updates	-	Intranet: • PENews • Did You Know • On the Frontpage	Ongoing (twice a week in four languages (DK, CN, US and DE)	All can contribute /Comm. Advisor

Figure 27. Example of a communication strategy. Source: Danfoss 2015.

Online training

Managers are often scattered geographically, and so online training is also held. It requires a different approach to the training, and so the content of the session is adapted to this form of training. For example, before the training, managers are asked to formulate their challenges in relation to leadership communication (see Figure 28 on page 132).

Based on the example's reflection questions, the trainer gets the opportunity to initiate a dialogue with the managers about their role. Along the way, there is also a small challenge in the form of a task where one of the participants, who has been notified in advance, must describe an abstract drawing that the other participants must draw. Then they talk about how difficult communication can be when you choose the wrong communication channel and along the way you don't ensure that the message is understood – like the Lego exercise that was described earlier.

During the training, participants are asked to work with a communication task that the advisor has defined, and the plan is devised as a group. The trainer fills out the template in the Leadership Communication Tool Kit on the basis of input from managers and at the same time asks participants detailed questions to challenge them on their use of the tool. In this way, the trainer ensures that the participants have benefited from the training.

Your input regarding communication challenge
– examples of input

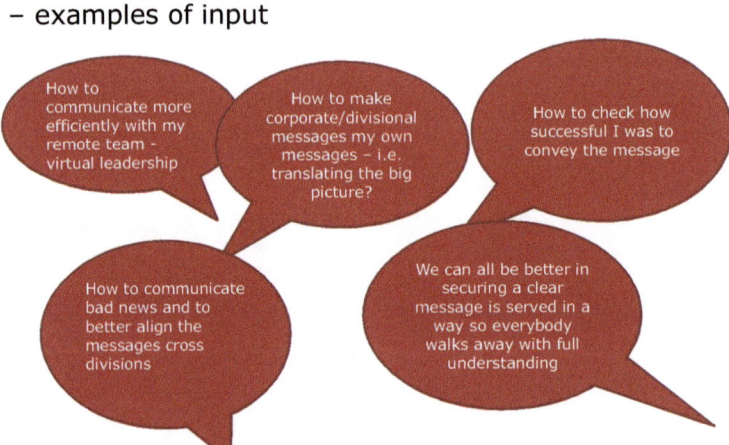

Figure 28. Example of managers' challenges in terms of leadership communication. Source: Danfoss.

Planning and implementation of communication training

The planning of the training is done in close collaboration with the HR department. HR partners are often close to individual managers. In some organizations they are on board when the individual manager's report from employee satisfaction surveys are reviewed, and improvement plans are being devised. In addition, they know the organization's various departments and are therefore crucial sparring partners for communication advisors when communication training must be planned and implemented.

In organizations where there is close collaboration between HR and management, HR partners can provide the communication advisor with a background on the managers and their challenges, which is useful for the advisor when he must plan and implement the training. If the organization is global, the local culture also plays a vital role. There is a big difference between training European, Asian and South and North American managers. Here it's again essential to have a close dialogue with HR, as they often have a good feel for managers' cultural differences.

For many communication advisors, the role of the trainer is new, and so a train-the-trainer concept can be a way to equip colleagues for the job. The concept is based on the communication advisors, who are more experienced in training, having a colleague along as a "trainee assistant" until the person in question feels adequately prepared to carry out the communication training on their own. The HR partners can also play a vital role here in that they can participate as observers during the training and give feedback to the trainer.

Chapter 11
Case: When the new strategy requires new communication skills

In 2010, Danfoss introduced a new strategy for the entire global group. The strategy was named Core & Clear. It set ambitious objectives and described how these objectives would be achieved by both divestments of businesses and radical improvements throughout the organization. The objective was to get back on track after the global crisis in 2008 and 2009, which affected the Group. It was also the beginning of a much more self-critical approach to implementing change in an organization which, according to Danfoss CEO Niels B. Christiansen, had become too complacent and lacked direction and discipline (Lunde 2015: 72, 79). Therefore, there was talk about fundamental changes to the entire organization, even when it came to self-perception and attitudes of managers and employees – perhaps one of the most significant changes in the company's (at the time) 77-year history.

The communications department faced the unprecedented task of equipping managers to communicate the new strategy in a way so that employees could follow the rationale and understand their own role in the new Danfoss. In other words, managers need to make the new strategy understandable for employees (dialogue) and then in an open dialogue with employees, give it meaning in the daily work (involvement).

The following section describes how all three forms of communication (transmission, dialogue and involvement) were put into play when the Core & Clear strategy had to be communicated. The forms of communication are regularly inserted in brackets and italics throughout the chapter (*transmission, dialogue, involvement*). Read more about the three forms of communication and the related paradigms in Chapters 5-7.

Despite the fact that the case describes leadership communication in a large global company, we hope it will also be an inspiration to those readers who work with leadership communication in other types of organizations.

Step 1: The strategy is launched
Transmission: The overall message

The Core & Clear strategy was launched at Danfoss' global management conference in January 2010 for 200 managers from the group's offices worldwide. Before that, senior management had involved a small group of senior managers for several months to ensure consensus on the new strategy and to create common ground. These managers would drive the implementation of the strategy, including the communication to 23,000 managers and employees throughout the global organization. Senior management's form of communication here was *involvement*, in that the strategy was formulated in collaboration with a group of managers so that they were prepared to convey the strategy. This gave the group of managers several months' head start over the rest of the organization (see Figure 6 in Chapter 3 with an example of how much of a head start management may have in relation to employees in change processes).

At the conference in January 2010, it was senior management and this group of highly-placed managers that via the forms of communication *dialogue and involvement* equipped the 200 participants to communicate the Core & Clear strategy to their employees. It was the beginning of the subsequent cascade communication throughout the group (read more about cascade communication in Chapter 3).

While managers attended the management conference, the group's 23,000 employees received the first information about the new strategy through the form of communication *transmission*. Articles on Danfoss' intranet, internal printed newsletters, as well as illustrations and short texts that presented the new strategy were displayed on all computers in the company – in the local language – both at offices and factories.

In the group's magazine, *Global Danfoss*, which was published for all employees (in nine languages), the elements of the strategy were reviewed. In his editorial, CEO Niels B. Christiansen explained that the strategy had been presented to managers and that they were now ready to discuss it with their employees when they returned from the conference. Christiansen also stressed in his editorial that "the agenda has been the biggest changes at Danfoss for many, many years – perhaps the biggest since the company was created 77 years ago" (Global Danfoss 2010). An expectation was created within the organization to hear more.

All 23,000 employees of the group also received a cube, along with *Global Danfoss*, with further details about the strategy in local languages:

Figure 29. Core & Clear cube with the strategy's key messages. Source: Global Danfoss 2010. Photo: Glenn Simonsen.

Senior management's message to all employees was repeated on the cube:

 Core & Clear will mean major changes for Danfoss. The new strategy will leave its mark throughout the company. However, most of us recognize the elements of Core & Clear, because the strategy focuses on implementing what we are good at, and to make it even better. (Global Danfoss 2010)

Immediately after the global management meeting, 12 senior managers travelled around to all Danfoss' companies worldwide to meet employees and communicate the new strategy. It was a journey that took 45 days to 46 factories and offices, where they presented the strategy 69 times. Here, too, the form of communication was *transmission*, in that senior managers held so-called balcony speeches to raise awareness of the strategy. It was the same messages on the new strategy that Niels B. Christiansen had given to the managers at the conference in January, and so in that way, everyone had received the same message.

To ensure that managers and employees understood the rationale behind the new strategy – and thus could later relate the decisions that would be taken to the strategy – the forms of communication *dialogue and involvement* were also put into play via cascade communication.

Figure 30. Senior management on the "soapbox". Niels B. Christiansen presents the new strategy to employees at the Danfoss factory in Gråsten, Denmark. Source: Danfoss Intranet 2010. Photo: Glenn Simonsen.

Step 2: Cascade communication
What does this mean for my team and me?

It was in the cascade communication that the form of communication went from *transmission* to *dialogue* and *involvement*.

It attracted much attention in the organization when senior management introduced the new strategy. The employees had been informed of the overall strategy and rationale behind it. Now it was up to the managers to put the strategy into a relevant context and together with the employees clarify what it meant for their daily work (*dialogue* and *involvement*). It was a task that would be driven by each senior manager team in the individual businesses in Danfoss, and where each manager – from middle managers to supervisors – would play a vital role.

Senior management of each business primarily prepared their managers for this job, and it meant that, together with the managers, they "translated" the strategy for their business area, so it made sense to the managers (*involvement*). The managers could then repeat this process with their employees and put into words what it meant for employees' daily work.

This process was fundamental, as it was the day-to-day managers who had to motivate employees to actively participate in the implementation of the strategy and maintain engagement from employees during the change process that lay ahead. It was a major communication task, especially since many employees were sceptical. Outsourcing of tasks and divesting businesses, which was part of the strategy, created a fear of redundancies among staff throughout the organization. During the crisis, they had been through several rounds of redundancies, and the message that new ways of working were to be introduced also caused turmoil. This fear of the future meant that there were still many possible interpretations among staff, and it was crucial that managers were aware of this.

The cascade process was implemented in all parts of the organization: The senior management teams in each of the five business areas and the six staff functions first put the strategy into a context that was relevant to the next level of management. They explained how the new strategy would come to influence their specific areas, including the new processes and working methods that would be introduced. This part of the process also included a dialogue with managers so that they were equipped to take the next step in the cascade: To communicate and establish a dialogue with their team and then with each employee about what the new strategy meant for the daily work and the plans going forward.

Large parts of the organization consisted of departments across many countries and cultures. Therefore, there was a need for detailed planning to reach out to all 23,000 employees from production workers at factories in China, Mexico, the United States and many parts of Europe, to development engineers worldwide, as well as salespeople in more than 50 countries. Everyone needed to understand the new strategy, and how they could help to achieve the ambitious objectives that senior management had set. The overall cascade process was illustrated as follows:

Figure 31. Cascade communication was both a top-down and bottom-up process. Source: Danfoss 2010.

The process had to be followed up by all management teams to ensure dialogue with all managers and employees. It ensured that managers at all levels had the opportunity to be equipped for the dialogue with their team, that the strategy made sense to all employees and that they understood what it meant for their daily work. The process also ensured that feedback was given from senior management to employees so that any "holes" in the communication could be rectified. The objective of this process was to create an open communication environment throughout the organization.

It was a major communication task, and each management team in the five business areas and the six staff functions had therefore initially engaged a communication advisor to assist them in planning and not least to equip managers to carry out the task.

At that time, Danfoss had not actively communicated Core & Clear externally, as senior management felt that it was important that employees understood the strategy and worked according to it in their daily work before it was communicated externally. The first step in the strategy was to get their house in order, i.e. to focus on core businesses and to ensure that internal processes and working methods were in place.

Staff throughout the group were involved in this work, and every time a decision was taken on the basis of the strategy, it was the managers' job to explain how it was connected with Core & Clear.

It soon became apparent that there was a need to better prepare managers for this job.

It was the beginning of the development of the Leadership Communication Tool Kit (see Chapter 9). In connection with the launch of the new communication tool, it also very quickly became apparent for the communication advisors that there was a need to train managers in the tool to improve their skills in leadership communication and to make them better at planning and implementing communication in their own team. The communication training concept was ready in spring 2011, and over the following years, hundreds of managers in the group were trained in the use of the Leadership Communication Tool Kit. You can read more about the training concept in Chapter 10.

Step 3: Example of leadership communication in a business division

To illustrate the process in connection with the launch of Core & Clear and the subsequent work to train managers and improve their communication skills, we will go through an example from one of Danfoss' business divisions, Danfoss Power Electronics. It was one of Danfoss' five divisions from 2010 to 2015, and it had approximately 4,000 employees worldwide.

The day after the Danfoss Group's global management conference in January 2010, the managers of Danfoss Power Electronics met to put the new Core & Clear strategy into a relevant context for the entire business division. In attendance were the 35 managers from Danfoss Power Electronics who had participated in the Danfoss Conference, and 35 additional top managers from the business area.

The President of Danfoss Power Electronics, Troels Petersen, had been in the group of managers who had been working on the strategy together with senior management, and now it was his job to communicate it to this group along with the 35 managers who had participated in the Danfoss Conference.

Therefore, he had given these 35 managers a task. They had to explain the new strategy to the managers who had not attended. Each of the 35 managers had been assigned one of the 35 newly arrived colleagues, and the evening before the meeting, they sat together in pairs and went through the strategy (*dialogue*). So, everybody had the same starting point to discuss and find out what the new strategy meant for the business division (*involvement*). At the meeting, the participants jointly formulated the messages that they had to communicate to employees (*dialogue*), and the process they had to review together with employees to jointly make sense of the strategy in relation to the daily work (*involvement*). They were given one month to communicate it to all 4,000 employees.

The planning continued in detail after the meeting in each department. It was a major job for many departments since it was not just a matter of sending out information, but it was also about entering into dialogue with the many middle managers who had not participated in the meeting. The strategy needed to make sense for these middle managers before they could communicate it to their team leaders and employees and help them to understand what it meant for their daily work. And as mentioned earlier, many – both managers and employees – were uncertain of the future after experiencing cuts during the crisis. This was also the case at Danfoss Power Electronics.

At that time, employees had only heard about the strategy from Danfoss' senior management. Therefore, there was a great need to understand what the strategy would specifically mean to the individual employee and the individual teams.

To meet this need, Troels Petersen sent a message to all employees while the management meeting at Danfoss Power Electronics was taking place. He announced that within the next month, their managers would give them more information about the strategy and in dialogue with them, clarify what it meant for their daily work. Videos were also released to the entire organization with interviews with managers who participated in the meeting (*transmission*).

Later, it was followed up on whether the cascade communication had been completed and feedback was given to senior management so that future communication could be adapted to the needs of the employees. This task was primarily driven by the communication advisor who worked closely with Troels Petersen and his management team.

Since 2010, Danfoss Power Electronics has continued to provide quarterly cascade communication, also when Ole Møller-Jensen took over as President of Danfoss Power Electronics in 2012. Via video (*transmission*) and online meetings (*dialogue*) with all middle managers around the world, they communicated the overall decisions, objectives and results, and so put the Core & Clear strategy into the business' fundamental context. Next, each member of senior management and his management team had the task of interpreting the overall messages based on their specific context (*involvement*) in order to equip their middle managers to communicate to their employees.

After each cascade communication, managers were asked to provide feedback from employees to management, so that they – also senior management – had a clear picture of how the messages were received, and so the communication could be adjusted. It was also crucial for senior management to have a close dialogue between middle managers to ensure the best possible communication with employees.

The feedback was collected for each function, and the management team in the function used it to improve their communication. An overall report was made by the communication advisor and presented to senior management, who then decided which communication measures they should focus on to create a common understanding of the decisions they had taken on the basis of the strategy.

To improve managers' communication, more than 500 manages in the Power Electronics Division throughout the world were trained in the Leadership Communication Tool Kit. The training took place face-to-face with up to 25 managers at a time. Sometimes it took place across departments, other times a department's management team gathered for training, especially when they faced a major communication task. In the global sales department, the training frequently took place online because managers are located throughout the world.

Feedback from managers has been very positive. "In Research & Development, many of our managers have completed communication training, both as individuals and together with their management team. It has undoubtedly given them a useful tool for improving their communication," said Søren Ejnar Nielsen, member of the management team in the development department.

Managers are responsible for communication

Is a communication advisor responsible for communication? The answer is clearly "no". Communication advisors are "midwives" when the key messages must be formulated, and they are also responsible for a communication *structure* that supports the business. At the same time, the advisor must ensure that managers are able to handle the communication task and that communication continuously improves. However, responsibility for communication lies with senior management and with the individual manager.

Therefore, it was clear from the start that Danfoss Power Electronics didn't want to establish its own communication department, but instead create a network of colleagues in the organization who worked determinedly on communication based on the overall communication structure/plan with a focus on ensuring excellent communication that is constantly improved in their respective areas.

Three roles were defined: communication ambassador, communication coordinator and intranet responsible.

The *communication ambassador*, who had overall responsibility for communication, was the senior manager of the function. It could, for example, be the manager of the global development and global sales department. All communication ambassadors were members of senior management in the division. Their role was to put communication on the agenda of the function's management team, to establish a structure that ensured that the key messages were cascaded in their department in an open communication environment, to participate in a communication audit (see the next section) and to subsequently follow up that ongoing improvements in communication were completed.

The *communication coordinator* was the right hand of the communication ambassador. Their role was to prepare the structure of the cascade communication, establish measures that would improve communication, including participation in audits and to ensure communication from the function's management team to the rest of the organization.

The role of the *intranet responsible* entailed continuous updating and development of the intranet function in collaboration with the communication coordinator.

This division of roles resulted in leadership communication in the division being tailored for the respective target groups, and managers received local help for communication.

Audits ensured continuous improvement

At the same time, every year a communication audit took place to ensure that all departments had prepared a communication structure/plan and translated it in practice, that excellent examples of communication measures were shared throughout the organization, managers were trained in communication and that there were adequate resources allocated to the communication task.

The audit was based on the results of the current employee satisfaction survey. After each audit, an action plan was drawn up for the next year to ensure continuous improvement of communication. At the next audit the year after, the plan was reviewed to ensure that all measures had been implemented, and if that was not the case, it was pointed out in the audit report and followed up.

The entire division was audited, and the senior manager from each department – from production, development, sales, to finance and HR – had responsibility for implementing the measures to improve communication and increase engagement among employees.

Audit process

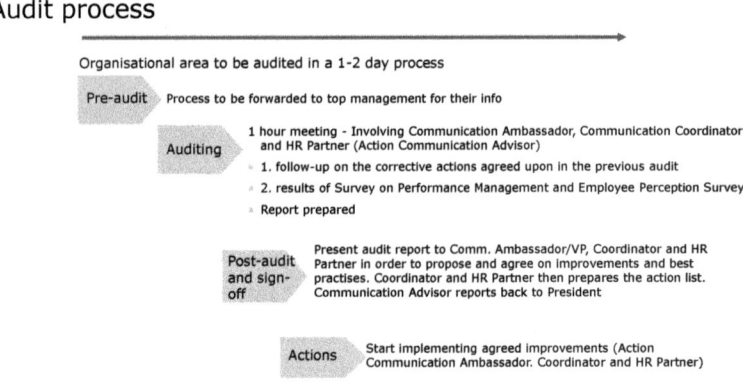

Figure 32. The audit process. Source: Danfoss 2011.

The audit process describes how each department is audited, and who is responsible for implementing the continuous improvement of internal communication, which is decided on the basis of the audit.

Hans Peter Boisen, who, among other things, had communication as his responsibility during these years, says of the audit process: "We took tools from work on quality and transformed them to also focus on ensuring the continuous improvement of communication in the division, and it has yielded excellent results".

From 2010-2015 – a time of considerable uncertainty due to the repercussions of the financial crisis and the profound change that the company underwent – the assessment of communication at Power Electronics increased in the employee satisfaction surveys conducted among employees.

Troels Petersen and Ole Møller-Jensen, who had both been Presidents of Danfoss Power Electronics from 2010-2015, and had spearheaded efforts to improve communication in the business, agree that a structured approach to leadership communication and an improvement in managers' skills in the communications field, had been crucial for the success they achieved in relation to communication at Power Electronics in a time that was marked by many changes.

Part III: Conclusion

By Marianne Wolff Lundholt and Anette Uldall

Conclusion

Despite the realization that leadership communication is important, there is a tendency for managers to give the task a lower priority. It can be the cause of poor performance for the company since communication is the key to motivating employees and thus to execute the objectives and strategy. Therefore, communication is an essential management tool.

We have defined the concept of "Leadership Communication" as follows:

> Leadership Communication should be understood as a task to facilitate activities and create an understanding of and ownership of the organization's strategy and also to provide employees with information about day-to-day activities.

In the book, we have looked at the opportunities and constraints inherent in leadership communication, which are essential for whether the communication is a success or a failure.

Leadership communication is undoubtedly a time-demanding task. There are many aspects that must be taken into account since communication is not only about what is being said or written, but also – and to a high degree – about how the message is interpreted by the recipients. Recipients usually have different backgrounds, personalities and experiences, and they may come from different cultures and interpret the message based on these factors. This is precisely what makes the task complex. As a manager, you may be amazed at how many different ways a message can be interpreted by employees. Therefore, it's essential that managers focus primarily on who is to receive the message and what you want to achieve with the communication – instead of immediately diving into formulating the text.

The message must also be relevant to employees to gain acceptance, and it requires that the manager knows their recipients, in other words, their target groups. It's also essential to gain insight into how a message is interpreted. It's an insight that the manager can use in their subsequent communication – partly to rectify any misunderstandings, and partly to use in other communication situations. However, it's our experience that many managers don't collect and use this knowledge that could otherwise improve their communication and thus the effect they achieve among employees.

We have also looked at the *advantages and limitations of cascade communication*. Communication, which comes from senior management and is cascaded to the organization, requires an extraordinary effort from senior management to succeed. It's senior management's job to communicate the key message and middle management's job to put these messages into a specific and relevant context for their employees so that they understand the message and take ownership if this is the objective. Middle managers play a vital role in cascade communication being successful and it is senior management's responsibility to equip middle managers to implement this communication task.

Based on what effect the manager wants to achieve with the communication, we have examined three *forms of communication*, each with its advantages and limitations. This approach provides a good starting point to understand the communication challenges that many organizations experience. At the same time, it becomes clear which levers the manager can adjust to improve the success rate of leadership communication. The key to good leadership communication depends on whether the manager is able to choose the form of communication that best serves the communication objective. It also depends on whether the manager can assess whether several of these forms of communication should come into play depending on the communication situation.

Transmission can be an excellent form of communication when it comes to transmitting a message, whereas *dialogue and involvement* are essential forms of communication when employees must understand the message or take ownership, for example, of a new way of working. In involvement, employees are involved, and together with the manager, they formulate the point of the change. When employees don't feel that they are involved in this interpretation, the manager may perceive employees as being opposed to change. However, most often, they are opposed to a lack of meaning. Therefore, involvement (the involvement paradigm) contains a significant and often untapped potential for leadership communication. The three forms of communication are summarized in the table below together with the communication objective, question, message and communication paradigm:

	Form of communication	Communication objective	Question	Message	Communication paradigm
1	Transmission from the manager to employees	Get knowledge of	Did you receive my message?	The message is formulated in advance of the communication	The information paradigm
2	Dialogue between the manager and employees	Have an opinion Changing behaviour	Did you understand my message?		The communication paradigm
3	Involvement of employees	Take ownership	How did you understand/ interpret my message?	The message is created in the communication situation in collaboration between the manager and employees	The involvement paradigm

Figure 33. Form of communication, communication objective, question, message and communication paradigm.

Rhetoric's three form of appeal, ethos, logos and pathos, can have a significant effect on recipients when they are used with care. They can be crucial to whether you convince recipients, and whether you establish a dialogue and an environment where employees feel they can freely express themselves. All elements must be considered in all three forms of communication.

Good leadership communication is not just about being prepared; it's also about which communication environment the manager has established – consciously or unconsciously. In a *closed communication environment*, employees are reluctant to give their views, which may be due to the management style. If critical feedback is not welcome, and you risk being labelled as someone who is combative when one expresses criticism, the manager has created an environment where employees' perception is that it's wiser to remain silent and signal that you consent. Most often employees in closed communication environments don't take ownership of a message, and it may have consequences for a company in the form of a lack of motivation and engagement, which in turn affects performance negatively. In a closed communication environment, it will be difficult for a manager to use the *dialogue* and *involvement* forms of communication, as these depend on whether employees are confident in entering into a dialogue with management.

An *open communication environment* is characterized by employee feedback being appreciated. Here the manager is authentic, i.e. true to themselves and their own beliefs, and with a high degree of credibility and thus has a high ethos. The manager openly shares information and their own opinions with employees, invites dialogue and is responsive. The authentic manager is a role model for employees who then dare to stand by their opinion and contribute with ideas and solutions.

We have also pointed out that social media is helping to open the communication environment, however, only when management takes the lead and uses these dialogue channels.

In the book's second part, we examined how managers can prepare communication with the help of a simple and effective tool, the Leadership Communication Tool Kit that consists of seven elements. Via the tool kit, managers go through a process in which they consider 1) the target group, 2) communication objectives – including the form of communication, 3) the message, 4) anticipated reactions, 5) channels, 6) timing and 7) responsibility for communication. In this way, they can adjust the message to the target group, which is crucial in order to succeed with leadership communication. It's our experience that with this tool in hand. managers become more effective and efficient in their preparation and so more confident that they are well prepared. They will be able to both plan a specific communication and devise a communication strategy for the organization, while they also develop their own communication skills.

Via examples in this book from private and public companies, we have described leadership communication in practice and in the book's last section, we have described a case from Danfoss. These examples and the Danfoss case are meant as inspiration for leadership communication in practice.

Bibliography

Aggerholm, H.K., B. Asmuß and M.G. Ditlevsen, et al. (2010). *Intern kommunikation under forandring*. Frederiksberg: Samfundslitteratur.

Argenti, P.A. (2017). Strategic Communication in the C-Suite. *International Journal of Business Communication*, 54(2): 146-160.

Ashcraft, K.L., T.R. Cooren Kuhn, F. (2009). Constitutional Amendments: "Materializing" Organizational Communication. *The Academy of Management Annals*, 3(1): 1-64.

Balmer, J. (2001). Corporate identity, corporate branding and corporate marketing. *European Journal of Marketing*, 35(3/4): 248-291.

Barge, J.K. and R.Y. Hirokawa (1989). Towards a communication competency model of leadership. *Small Group Behavior*, 20(2): 167-189.

Becker-Jensen, L. (2001). *Den sproglige dåseåbner – om at formidle faglig viden forståeligt*. Frederiksberg: Roskilde University Press.

Bordum, A. (2016). "Strategisk Ledelseskommunikation". I: J. Helder and J.L. Nørgaard (ed.), *Kommunikationsteori – en grundbog*, 2nd edition. Copenhagen: Hans Reitzels Forlag: 269-283.

Bowen, F. and K. Blackmon (2003). Spirals of Silence: The Dynamic Effects of Diversity on Organizational Voice. *Journal of Management Studies*, 40(6): 1393-1417.

Christensen, J.H. (2010). *Når forretningen kommunikerer*. Copenhagen: Gyldendal Business.

Cornelissen, J. (2017). *Corporate Communication*. London: Sage.

Craig, R.T. (1999). Communication Theory as a Field. *Communication Theory*, 9(2): 119-161.

Daft, R.L. and R.H. Lengel (1986). Organizational information requirements, media richness and structural design. *Management Science*, 32(5): 554-571.

Danfoss A/S (2010). *Global Danfoss 1/2010*.

Dent, E.B. and S.G. Goldberg (1999). Challenging "Resistance to Change". *The Journal of Applied Behavioral Science*, 35(1): 25-41.

Dundon, T. and P. Gollan (2007). Re-conceptualising non-union voice. *International Journal of Human Resource Management*, 18(7): 1182-1198.

Eylon, D. and K.Y. Au (1999). Exploring empowerment cross-cultural differences along the power distance dimension. *International Journal of Intercultural Relations*, 23(3): 373-385.

Foster, D. and J. Jonker (2005). Stakeholder relationships: the dialogue of engagement. *Corporate Governance: The international journal of business in society*, 5(5): 51-57.

Friedl, J. and A. Verčič (2011). Media preferences of digital natives' internal communication: A pilot study. *Public Relations Review*, 37(1): 84-86.

Gifford, J. (2013). Social Technology, Social Business? *CIPD Survey Report*. https://www.cipd.co.uk/Images/social-technology-social-business_2013_tcm18-10323.pdf (downloaded 19.12.17).

Greve, L. and S. Hildebrandt (2012). [*Transformational leadership communication – metaphors in organizations*] *Forandrende ledelseskommunikation – metaforer i organisationer*. Frederiksberg: Samfundslitteratur.

Guldbrandsen, I.T. and S.N. Just (2011). The collaborative paradigm: towards an invitational and participatory concept of online communication. *Media, Culture & Society*, 33(7): 1095-1108.

Hallahan, K.D., D. Holtzhausen and B.v. Ruler, et al. (2007). Defining Strategic Communication. *International Journal of Strategic Communication*, 1(1): 3-35.

Hammer, S. and J. Høpner (2014). *Meningsskabelse, organisering og ledelse*. Frederiksberg: Samfundslitteratur.

Hart, S. and R. Quinn (1993). Roles Executives Play: CEOs, Behavioral Complexity, and Firm Performance. *Human Relations*, 46(5): 543-574.

Harter, J.K., F.L. Schmidt and T.L. Hayes (2002). Business unit-level relationship between employee satisfaction, employee engagement, and business outcomes: A meta-analysis. *Journal of Applied Psychology*, 87(2): 268-279.

Hennestad, B.W. (1990). The symbolic impact of double bind leadership. *Journal of Management Studies*, 27(3): 265-280.

Hofstede, G. (1991). *Cultures and organizations: software of the mind*. New York: McGraw-Hill.

Holmgren, J. and O.U. Friis (2014). [*Study of strategy work in Danish companies*] *Undersøgelse af strategiarbejdet i danske virksomheder: Faglig rapport*. Herning: AU Herning, Business and Social Science.

Huang, J., J. Baptista and R.D. Galliers (2013). Reconceptualizing rhetorical practices in organizations: The impact of social media on internal communications. *Information & Management*, 50: 112-124.

Huang, X., E.V. d.Vliert and G.V. d.Vegt (2005). Breaking the Silence Culture: Stimulation of Participation and Employee Opinion Withholding Cross-nationally. *Management and Organization Review*, 1(3): 459-482.

Huy, Q and A. Shipilov (2012). The Key to Social Media Success Within Organizations. *MIT Sloan Management Review*, 54(1): 72-82.

Johnsen, E. (1997). "Ledelseskommunikation". I: E. Johnsen and S. Hildebrandt (ed.), *Ledelse '97*. Copenhagen: Børsens Forlag: 85-119.

Johnsen, E. (2003). "Ledelseskommunikation". I: J. Helder and B. Kragh (ed.), *Når virksomheden åbner sit vindue*. Frederiksberg: Samfundslitteratur: 168-178.

Johnsen, E. (2009). "Ledelseskommunikation". I: J. Helder, T. Bredenlöw and J.L. Nørgaard (ed.), *Kommunikationsteori: en grundbog*. Copenhagen: Hans Reitzels Forlag: 291-303.

Kalla, H.K. (2005). Integrated internal communications: a multidisciplinary perspective. *Corporate Communications: An International Journal*, 10(4): 302-314.

Kim, Y., D. Sohn and S.M. Choi (2011). Cultural difference in motivations for using social network sites: A comparative study of American and Korean college students. *Computers in Human Behavior*, 27(1): 365-372.

Kipnis, D. and S.M. Schmidt (1988). Upward influence styles: Relationship with performance evaluations, salary, and stress. *Administrative Science Quarterly*, 33(4): 528-542.

Kjærbeck, S. and M.W. Lundholt (2018a). Conflicting perspectives in a housing association: An investigation of employees' counter-narratives in relation to a new business strategy. *Journal of Organizational Change Management.* https://doi.org/10.1108/JOCM-12-2016-0259

Kjærbeck, S. and M.W. Lundholt (2018b). "Communicating business strategy to employees: can dialogue be part of the show?", conference presentation, March.

Knoll, M. and R. van Dick (2013). Do I Hear the Whistle...? A First Attempt to Measure Four Forms of Employee Silence and Their Correlates. *Journal of Business Ethics,* 113(2): 349-362.

Larkin, T.J. and S. Larkin (2006). *Communicating Big Change Using Small Communication.* New York: Larkin Communication Consulting. http://www.larkin.biz/data/Communicating_Big_Change-English.pdf (downloaded 15.01.18).

Larson, G.S. and G.L. Pepper (2003). Strategies for Managing Multiple Organizational Identifications: A Case of Competing Identities. *Management Communication Quarterly,* 16(4): 528-557.

Lewis, D. (1992). Communicating organizational culture. *Australian Journal of Communication,* 19(2): 47-57.

Lin, S. and R.E. Johnson (2015). A Suggestion to Improve a Day Kees Your Depletion Away: Examining Promotive and Prohibitive Voice Behaviors Within a Regulatory Focus and Ego Depletion Framework. *Journal of Applied Psychology,* 100(5): 1381-1397.

Liu, S., J. Liao and H. Wei (2015). Authentic Leadership and Whistleblowing: Mediating Roles of Psychological Safety and Personal Identification. *Journal of Business Ethics,* 131(1): 107-119.

Lunde, N. (2015). *Det ny Danfoss – Sådan forvandlede Niels B. Christiansen landets største industrivirksomhed.* Copenhagen: Gyldendal.

Lundholt, M.W. (2017a). Virksomhedens sande ansigt. *Marketcommunity.com.* http://www.marketcommunity.com/Content/articles/MARKET-96-Identitet-Vaerdier/Virksomhedens-sande-ansigt (downloaded 15.01.18).

Lundholt, M.W. (2017b). Modhistorier – fra barriere til ressource? *Symboløkonomiske Nyheder* 7. https://issuu.com/pernillerm/docs/brandbase_07 (downloaded 15.01.18).

Lundholt, M.W. and A. Uldall (2010). *Management Communication Tool Kit.* Danfoss A/S.

Lundholt, M.W. and T. Dalager (2017). What's the point? *Workshop for managers at Danfoss.*

Marques, J.F. (2010). Enhancing the Quality of Organizational Communication. *Journal of Communication Management,* 14(1): 47-58.

Maturana, H.R and F. Varela (1987). *The Tree of Knowledge: The Biological Roots of Human Understanding.* Boston: New Science Library.

Maxfield, D. (2016). How a Culture of Silence Eats Away at Your Company. *Harvard Business Review.* 7 December. https://hbr.org/2016/12/how-a-culture-of-silence-eats-away-at-your-company (downloaded 19.12.17).

McPhee, R.D. and P. Zaug (2000). The Communicative Constitution of Organizations: A Framework for Explanation. *The Electronic Journal of Communication,* 10(1/2): 1-16.

Mehrabian, A. (1981). *Silent Messages: Implicit Communication of Emotions and Attitudes,* 2nd edition. Belmont, CA: Wadsworth.

Men, L.R. (2014). Internal Reputation Management: The Impact of Authentic Leadership and Transparent Communication. *Corporate Reputation Review*, 17(4): 254-272.

Monzani, L., S. Braun and R. Dick (2016). It takes two to tango: The interactive effect of authentic leadership and organizational identification on employee silence intentions. *German Journal of Human Resource Management*, 30(3-4): 246-266.

Morrison, E.W. and F.J. Milliken (2000). Organizational Silence: A Barrier to Change and Development in a Pluralistic World. *The Academy of Management Review*, 25(4): 706-725.

Nielsen, M.F. (2010a). *Strategisk kommunikation*. Copenhagen: Akademisk Forlag.

Nielsen, M.F. (2010b). *Fortolkningsledelse: mellemledernes kommunikative arbejde med værdier og kulturskabelse*. Frederiksberg: Samfundslitteratur.

Nielsen, M.F. (2014). *Strategisk kommunikation*, 2nd edition. Copenhagen: Akademisk Forlag.

O'Murchú, L. (2015). "Set Yourself Up for Success, Four Steps to Effective Internal Communication". I: K. Ruck (ed.), *Exploring Internal Communication. Towards Informed Employee Voice*. Dorchester: Gower: 95-103.

O'Rourke, J.S. (2014). "Management Communication in Transition". I: J.S. O'Rourke (ed.), *Management Communication*. Harlow: Pearson: 1-27.

Petersen, H. (2000). *Forandringskommunikation*. Frederiksberg: Samfundslitteratur.

Phillips, L. (2011). *The Promise of Dialogue. The dialogic turn in the production and communication of knowledge*. Amsterdam/Philadelphia: John Benjamins.

Project Management Institute (PMI) (2013). *A guide to the Project Management Body of Knowledge (PMBOK guide)*, 5th edition. Newtown Square: Project Management Institute.

Rasmus, D.W. (2011). Enterprise Social Networking: Finding Value in Serendipity. *Danielwrasmus.com*. https://blogs.office.com/wp-content/uploads/sites/14/Enterprise-Social-Networking-Value.pdf (downloaded 20.12.17).

Rawlins, B. (2008). Measuring the Relationship Between Organizational Transparency and Employee Trust. *Public Relations Journal*, 2(2): 1-21.

Riel, C.B.M. (1992). *Principles of Corporate Communication*. London: Prentice Hall.

Riel, C.B.M. and C.J. Fombrun (2007). *Essentials of corporate communication: implementing practices for effective reputation management*. London: Routledge.

Riel, C.B.M. (2016). "Corporate Communication – et integreret perspektiv". I: J. Helder and J. L. Nørgaard (ed.), *Kommunikationsteori - en grundbog*, 2nd edition. Copenhagen: Hans Reitzels Forlag: 283-303.

Ruben, B.D. and R.A. Gigliotti (2016). Leadership as Social Influence: An Expanded View of Leadership Communication Theory and Practice. *Journal of Leadership & Organizational Studies*, 23(4): 467-479.

Ruck, K. (2015). "Informed Employee Voice". I: Ruck, K. (ed.), *Exploring Internal Communication: Towards Informed Employee Voice*. London: Gower: 47-57.

Saint-Exupéry, A. de. (2017 [1943]). The Little Prince. Copenhagen: Lindhardt & Ringhof.

SDU (2016). *Emergency contingency film*. http://www.sdu.dk/Om_SDU/Beredskab_paa_SDU/Informationsmateriale/Beredskabsfilm (downloaded 15.01.18).

Tourish, D. (1998). The God that failed: replacing false messiahs with open communication. *Australian Journal of Communication*, 25(2): 99-114.

Tourish, D. and O. Hargie (2004). "Motivating critical upward communication: a key challenge for management decision making". I: D. Tourish and O. Hargie (ed.), *Key Issues in Organisational Communication*. London: Routledge.

Tourish, D. and P. Robson (2006). Sensemaking and the Distortion of Critical Upward Communication in Organizations. *Journal of Management Studies*, 43(4): 711-730.

Truss, K., E. Soane and C. Edwards, et al. (2006). *Working Life: Employee Attitudes and Engagement*. Wimbledon: CIPD.

Tsoukas, H. (2009). A Dialogical Approach to the Creation of New Knowledge in Organizations. *Organization Science*, 20(6): 941-957.

Vakola, M. and D. Bouradas (2005). Antecedents and consequences of organisational silence: an empirical investigation. *Employee Relations*, 27(5): 441-458.

Version2. (2016). IT-chefer fortæller ikke topledelsen om brud på datasikkerheden. *Version2*. https://www.version2.dk/artikel/it-chefer-fortaeller-ikke-topledelsen-om-brud-paa-datasikkerheden-820245 (downloaded 20.12.17).

Walumbwa, F.O., P. Wang and H. Wang, et al. (2010). Psychological processes linking authentic leadership to follower behaviors. *The Leadership Quarterly*, 21: 901-914.

Weick, K.E. (1995). *Sensemaking in Organizations*. London: Sage.

Welch, M. (2015). "Dimensions of Internal Communication and Implications for Employee Engagement". I: K. Ruck (ed.), *Exploring Internal Communication. Towards Informed Employee Voice*. Dorchester: Gower: 25-37.

Westley, F. and H. Mintzberg (1989). Visionary leadership and strategic management. *Strategic Management Journal*, 10 (special issue): 17-32.

Wright, M. (2017). The 3 keys to IC success in 2017. *Simplycommunicate.com*. https://simply-communicate.com/three-keys-to-ic-success-in-2017 (downloaded 20.12.17).

Zerfass, A. and M. Sherzada (2015). Corporate communications from the CEO's perspective: How top executives conceptualize and value strategic communication. *Corporate Communications: An International Journal*, 20(3): 291-309.